THE ONCE-UBIQUITOUS
PADDLE STEAMER

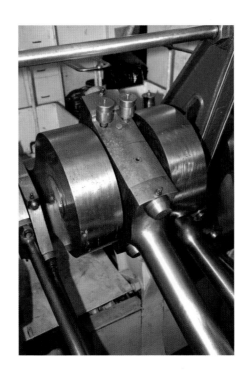

JOHN HANNAVY

First published in Great Britain in 2014

Copyright © 2014 John Hannavy.
www.johnhannavy.co.uk

A CIP catalogue record for this book is available from the British Library.

John Hannavy has asserted his right under the Copyright, Designs and Patents Act 1988 to be identified as the author of this book.

ISBN 978 0 85710 092 4

PiXZ Books
Halsgrove House, Ryelands Business Park,
Bagley Road, Wellington, Somerset TA21 9PZ
Tel: 01823 653777
Fax: 01823 216796
email: sales@halsgrove.com

An imprint of Halstar Ltd, part of the Halsgrove group of companies
Information on all Halsgrove titles is available at: www.halsgrove.com

Printed and bound in China by Everbest Printing Co Ltd

Front cover image: PS *Maid of the Loch* – the largest paddle steamer ever to sail on a British inland waterway – is undergoing restoration at Balloch Pier on Loch Lomond. This view was taken in the mid 1990s.
Title page image: A detail of the PS *Waverley*'s engine, built by Rankin & Blackmore of Greenock.
Contents page image: A few of the hundreds of thousands of 'Edmondson' tickets issued from David MacBrayne's quayside offices on Scotland's west coast.

Permission to use illustrations from the following photographers and collections is acknowledged with thanks: Blackgang Chine World of Imagination 93, 119: Cyril Perrier Collection, courtesy of Tom Lee 44 bottom, 128; Noel Donnelly 12; Felixstowe Museum 141; From originals in the Glasgow School of Art Archives 94, 104, 105 top; Michael Hallett 83; John Hannavy 10 bottom, 11 top, 13 bottom, 18-19, 26-7, 31, 44, 46-7, 73 top & middle, 74 top, 75 bottom, 76 bottom, 79 bottom, 90, 91 bottom, 103 bottom left, 104, 105 bottom, 124 main picture, 129-131, 133 bottom; Mike Hickey 89 middle, 140; Sean Mack through Wikipedia Commons 30; Markham Grange Museum 103, 137; Medway Maritime Trust 10, 139; Paddle Steamer Preservation Society 79 bottom left; Pembrokeshire County Archives 135-137; Pembrokeshire County Archives/Brace Family 134; San Francisco Maritime Historic National Park 11, 76; Scottish Maritime Museum 44 top, 45; Wessex Archaeology, Crown Copyright 34 bottom, 35. All other historic images are from the author's own collection and from private collections.

Thanks for their support and input to John Beveridge, Noel Donnelly, Andrew Gladwell, Michael Hallett, Phil Harding, Tom Lee, David Mann and the staff of the Scottish Maritime Museum, and everyone else who has added to the story along the way.

CONTENTS

INTRODUCTION

THERE IS A LOVELY STORY, probably apocryphal, which I was told many years ago while visiting a soon-to-be-restored paddle steamer, then being prepared as a static visitor attraction to help raise much-needed funds. The volunteer showing me around had, reportedly, overheard a zealous Health and Safety inspector advising a member of the preservation trust that, in order to get insurance for visitors coming on board, those 'humps' in the passageway flooring either side of the engine room would have to be levelled off. It would be, apparently, a safety risk having visitors climbing over them.

When it was explained to him that without those 'humps', the boat would never be going anywhere, as they carried the drive-shafts to the paddles, the inspector admitted to knowing very little about how a paddle steamer worked. All he was concerned about, apparently, was the risk of a visitor tripping over the steps, adding to his concerns about the impossibility in getting wheelchairs over them without very long gradually inclined ramps!

Not much more than half a century ago, excursion paddle steamers were still a common sight plying the lakes, lochs, rivers and coastal resorts of Britain. Most people were sufficiently familiar with them to have at least a basic under-

The May 27 1892 issue of the journal *Engineering* included this illustration of the engines for PS *Koh-i-noor*, built by Fairfield Shipbuilding & Engineering Ltd's works at Govan for the Victoria Steam-boat Association. The two-cylinder diagonal compound engines had an indicated 3,500 horse-power, and during her trials the 944grt, 300ft long steamer achieved just under 20 knots over a measured mile. Her near-identical sister ship, PS *Royal Sovereign*, joined the fleet in the following year, fitted with identical engines.

standing of how they worked! Children of all ages marvelled at the polished brass on the engines – often visible through glass panels – and the crew members working away below.

In my own Scottish childhood, visits to my grandparents involved crossing the Tay on either the 1924-built paddler *Sir William High*, or the 1929-built *B.L.Nairn* – both built by Caledon of Dundee – the former operating until 1951, the latter until 1966, the crossing spent peering down below to watch what we called the 'sweeper engines'. *B.L.Nairn* was, in fact, the last paddle steamer to be launched from the Caledon yard. A highlight of the school summer holidays was a trip 'Doon the Watter' on one of the Clyde paddlers which worked into the mid 1960s.

The golden age of the excursion paddle steamer coincided with the golden age of the picture postcard in the years before the Great War, so the many hundreds of vessels which worked out of Britain's river and coastal ports were the subject of beautifully tinted postcards.

It is, perhaps, difficult today to grasp the importance and the popularity of passenger paddle steamer services, but the sheer number of vessels which were built and operated in the closing quarter of the 19th century and the first decades of the 20th attest to that popularity.

Clyde yards built a substantial percentage of them – famous shipyards such as Inglis, Fairfield's of Govan, and others working hard to meet the growing demand for excursion ships. 'Clyde-built' was a by-word for quality, so steamers from Scottish yards were much in demand all around the British Isles. Steamer companies vied with each other to offer the fastest, the biggest, the most luxurious services, and some truly magnificent vessels were launched into the river.

It was the Fairfield yard which built two of the finest Edwardian steamers – *Koh-i-noor* and *Royal Sovereign* for Palace Steamers. They worked the routes from London Bridge to Clacton and other resorts on the south east coast, and were fitted with funnels which could be lowered to allow them to pass beneath the bridge.

By the 1950s, with the increase in motoring holidays, the popularity of the excursion steamer trip was already waning, and by the 1960s few were making any money.

And then suddenly, just like steam trains, they had almost all gone – victims of the growing popularity of the motor car, cheap flights and more sophisticated holiday expectations – and we had barely noticed.

No more than a decade later, there were none left operating, except for the *Waverley*. And without her team of willing volunteers, even she would have been long gone.

By the early 1970s, most had been broken up, but a few lucky vessels survived, thanks to the tenacity and effort of

Below: This beautifully tinted postcard from c.1903 attests to the popularity of paddle steamer services to the Isle of Man. The 2140grt PS *Empress Queen* was built in 1897 by Fairfields of Govan for the Isle of Man Steam Packet Company, and operated services between Liverpool and Douglas until requisitioned by the War Office as a troop carrier in early 1915. Her passenger capacity was 1994, and, judging by the crowds, she had arrived fully laden on the day this photograph was taken. She was abandoned after running aground off the Isle of Wight on 1 February 1916.

Passengers arriving at Douglas, I.O.M., from Liverpool, by the "Empress Queen."

volunteer trusts. Several of those lucky few have since, sadly, also been lost. Some got very close to preservation, but were lost when even relatively small sums of money to save them could not be raised. The story of one such vessel, the PS *Menna*, built for a ferry service across the Menai Straits, is told later in this book.

Even as late as the 1990s when the National Historic Ships Register – now National Historic Ships UK – was first set up, there were quite a few more surviving paddle steamers than there are today. And given its terms of reference, they should still be with us.

The first paragraph of the register's terms of reference states that its remit is "To act as the primary source of independent and objective advice to the Secretary of State for Culture, Olympics, Media and Sport, other government departments, and the Devolved Administrations, on all matters relating to historic ships, with particular regard to conservation, preservation, restoration, reconstruction, adaptation, replication, operation, and maintenance: [to advise on the vessels'] heritage, social, and economic value," and their "educational potential as a resource for greatly enlarging public understanding of the naval, maritime, social and economic histories of these islands."

Very commendable, but the economics of preserving and operating a large ship are very different to the cost challenges of preserving a steam launch, a steam locomotive, or a traction engine, and the best intentions and hard work of volunteers are sometimes not enough.

That proved to be the case with the Humber ferry PS *Lincoln Castle*, built in 1940 by A. & J. Inglis at Pointhouse on the Clyde (Yard No. 1024) with triple expansion diagonal engines by Ailsa Shipbuilding Co. of Troon. After years as a floating bar in Grimsby, she was broken in 2010, but even after demolition had started, plans were announced – which always looked wildly ambitious – to rebuild her on to a new steel hull and return her to operational condition by 2014. That of course never happened, with Historic Ships UK lamenting at the time that it had no statutory powers which it could have used to stop the vessel's demolition.

The issue appeared partly to hinge on the fact that at high tide she floated, and was therefore not a static object. Had

she been static, there were powers which might have been invoked to prevent her destruction while the embryonic preservation group continued to raise the necessary funds to save her. In 2010 they already had pledges of over £100,000, but the vessel's owners refused to sell her to the group.

When National Historic Ships UK was set up in 2006, there were still nine historic paddlers surviving in British waters, albeit some of them in a parlous state. There are currently only seven of them left, and at the time of writing only two of those are still sailing. They are the 1947-built *Waverley* and the Dartmouth-built excursion steamer *Kingswear Castle* which has recently returned to work on the River Dart after many years sailing on the Medway.

The steam tug *John H Amos* – built by Bow McLachlan & Co. of Paisley in 1931 – is out of the water and sitting on a floating pontoon. She is in the early stages of an extensive restoration at Chatham, with long-term plans to return her to steam.

The former Humber ferry PS *Wingfield Castle* is a static exhibit in Hartlepool, back at the yard where she was built by William Gray & Company in 1934, while one of her sister ships, also 1934-built by Gray, the PS *Tattershall Castle* – still with her original engine, but heavily modified from her days plying the Humber Estuary – is moored on the Thames as a floating bar and restaurant.

Built as PS *Chancellor* for the Loch Long & Lochgoil Steamboat Company in 1864, the 152grt PS *Shandon* was a regular sight at Glasgow's Broomielaw in the 1880s and early 1890s, operating a service to Rothesay for Captain William Buchanan. Built by Blackwood & Gordon at their Castle Street yard in Port Glasgow, she had been broken up several years before this postcard view was published in 1902. As PS *Daniel Adamson* she spent her final months on the Manchester Ship Canal but that proved not to be commercially viable. She was broken up in late1895.

Above: The paddle tug PS *John H Amos* is currently awaiting restoration on a pontoon at Chatham.

Right: The hawsers on the steam winch at Balloch, Loch Lomond. The slipway, carriage and pier, built by George Halliday of Rothesay in 1902, cost £8154.4s.2d., while the twin horizontal single-expansion steam engine, built by John Bennie at Glasgow's Star Works, cost £1150.0s.6d. Today steam is raised in a vertical 1953 boiler which was originally from a steam crane. Restoring the facility in 2006 cost over £600,000. The earlier boiler had come from a steam locomotive. With this winch, PS *Maid of the Loch* was successfully hauled out of the loch for inspection on 27 June 2006. Winches like this were once commonplace, but this one is now unique.

PS *Wingfield Castle* still has her original engines – built by Central Marine Engine Works in West Hartlepool – but as the lock gates through which she entered the docks have been narrowed since her arrival in 1991, she is unlikely ever to use them again.

Medway Queen – built in 1924 at the Ailsa Shipyard in Troon – is being rebuilt in Gillingham, her new hull having been completed in Bristol in 2013. It is hoped she will be returned to steam on the Medway at some time in the not-too-distant future, thanks to energetic fund-raising by the Medway Queen Preservation Trust, and a major grant from the Heritage Lottery Fund.

The 1953-built PS *Maid of the Loch* – the last large excursion paddle steamer to be built in Britain and the biggest ever to sail on any British lake or loch – is currently undergoing restoration at Balloch on Loch Lomond, but in need of £3.3M to complete the task. The steam-powered slipway at Balloch has been restored and returned to use, and it is hoped that sufficient funding to complete the restoration of the steamer will be achieved soon. Plans to steam her in 2013 – her 60th birthday – proved years too optimistic. The fights to save others – most recently the PS *Ryde* – have inevitably ended at the breakers yard.

Two more British-built paddlers survive abroad. The PS *Princess Elizabeth*, built in 1927 by Day, Summers & Company of Southampton, and one of the many paddle steamers in the flotilla which carried out the Dunkirk rescue in 1940, is berthed, fittingly, in Dunkerque and used as a conference centre. She had a long career as an excursion ship out of Bournemouth and Southampton.

Above: The funnels of PS *Waverley*, at her home berth on the Clyde adjacent to Glasgow's Science Centre.

Perhaps a greater loss to the small number of steam vessels which can be seen in Britain, and which ought to have been preserved in British waters, the steam paddle tug *Eppleton Hall*, built for the Lambton & Hetton Colliery Company by Hepple & Co. of South Shields in 1914, and the last surviving example of a Tyne paddle tug, is in America.

She is in San Francisco at Hyde Street Pier – part of the Maritime Historical National Park – and showing the effects

Left: The 166grt PS *Eppleton Hall* arriving at her new home in San Francisco's Maritime Historic National Park, 24 March, 1970. Restored in Sunderland in 1969 and converted to oil burning, she crossed the Atlantic under her own steam, powered by two original side-lever condensing engines.

11

At least seven paddle vessels have been named PS *Monarch*. The first was a 295grt steamer for the Hull-Hamburg route, built at Thorne of Goole in 1830. *Monarch* (II) was the 1833 88grt wooden tug built by Edward Robson of South Shields, seen towing HMS *Temeraire* in J. M. W. Turner's painting. She had a single cylinder engine by H. S. Wait of North Shields. The 128grt *Monarch* (III) was built by Barr & McNab of Renfrew in 1846 and sailed on the Clyde until sold to Tasmania in 1854. *Monarch* (IV) of 1871 was another South Shields-built tug. *Monarch* (V), the 315grt excursion steamer, above, was built at the Blackwall yard of R. & H. Green in 1888 for Cosens & Company, spending her entire 62 years under their flag. Intended for cross-Channel service, she spent most of her working life operating excursions between Swanage and Bournemouth, where she is seen here c.1903. Her replacement, the 1924-built 412grt PS *Shanklin* was renamed *Monarch* and became the last paddler to join the Cosens fleet.

Right: PS *Monarch* (VII) returns to the water at Poole, August 2013.

of lack of attention. Many features of the design of the *John H Amos* can be seen in this little craft, despite her being nearly twenty years older. In many respects *John H Amos* was already well out of date when she was launched in 1931.

The little 1984-built and Dorset-based PS *Monarch* – at least the seventh paddler to carry that name – is, at the time of writing, the third of a trio of operational paddlers in Britain.

It is to be hoped that those paddle steamers which are currently being restored or rebuilt – *Medway Queen, Maid of the Loch* and *John H Amos* – are all eventually returned to steam, and I look forward to travelling on them when those days come.

Eppleton Hall and *John H Amos* are the only surviving examples of the many hundreds of paddle tugs – a lot of them clinker-built wooden vessels – which worked the ports around Britain's coast for over a hundred years. These powerful little craft, often doubling as excursion steamers in the summer months, had working lives very much longer than the majority of the larger and much more famous

pleasure boats. *Medway Queen* and *Maid of the Loch* each has its own important place in the history of the British paddle steamer.

Many of the finest Edwardian excursion steamers were featured in the millions of postcards produced for the tourist market. A number of those cards – beautifully tinted and printed at a very high quality – form the basis of many of the illustrations in this book. The finest often came from print works in Saxony, Bavaria and Belgium in the years before the First World War. During and after the war, German-printed cards lost much of their popularity.

Above: An 1888 engraving based on Turner's famous painting 'The Fighting Temeraire'. The steam paddle tug *Monarch* (II) hired from the Thames Steam Towing Company is seen towing the great wooden warship up the Thames to the breakers in 1838.

This book does not set out to be a comprehensive history of the paddle steamer – there are many people much better qualified to write such volumes. Rather it offers a series of snapshots of the fascinating story and enduring charm of the paddler steamer over the last two hundred years illustrated by historic images and my own contemporary photography.

It also offers a look at those few precious survivors of the age of the excursion steamer, the ferry and of the paddle tug, and the efforts of those whose passion is to keep them alive and steaming.

I am indebted to the operators and volunteers on these steamers for the manner in which they have generously given of their time and expertise – not to mention the sheer pleasure they have given me exploring the vessels while they do what they were built for. My thanks too to everyone who has loaned me photographs or provided snippets of information for inclusion in this book. I hope I have made good use of all your help and guidance.

John Hannavy, 2014

Below left: The port paddle box of PS *Waverley* – Britain's best-known paddle steamer.

Below: The bows of PS *Monarch* (VII) as she appeared before her 2013 restoration. Her name is now carried on her paddle boxes.

THE STEAMER RESCUE
THAT NEVER HAPPENED

ON 30 JUNE 1923 on the banks of the River Dee in North Wales, Mrs A. H. Richards, the wife of the former Mayor of Caernarfon, launched the paddle steamer ferry PS *Menna*, built to join the 1896 Clyde-built PS *Arvon* on the route between Caernarfon and Tal Y Foel on Anglesey. After the launch, a presentation was made to Mrs Richards to commemorate the event, and while the gift she received – probably a small silver mallet mounted on a plinth – has been lost over time, the 90mm x 50mm silver plaque which was once affixed to the plinth has survived. The steamer herself is long gone.

Above: The engraved plaque which was once attached to the gift presented to Mrs Richards on launch day. Just before launch, permission to register the vessel as PS *Menai* was refused and she was actually named *Menna*. Mrs Richards' plaque, however, had already been engraved.

Right: These plans for the vessel were almost certainly redrawn long after the steamer was built. On the drawings she is identified as the SS *Menna*. Her dimensions were 80 feet long, 17ft 6ins beam and 30ft 6ins across the sponsons. The original plans were destroyed in a firebomb attack on the James Street, Liverpool, premises of the ship's consultant engineers, Alexander Esplen & Company, in 1941.

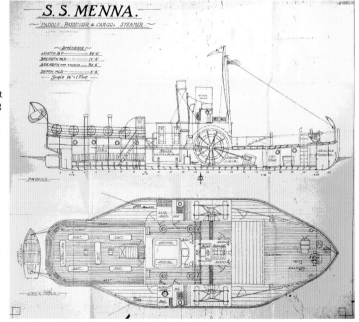

Left: PS *Alumchine* crossing the River Cleddau between Pembroke and Neyland in the late 1930s. A large box structure appears behind the paddle box which has gone in later images. PS *Alumchine* could carry five vehicles at a time; the bridge carries more than 10,000 vehicles a day. The service was eventually withdrawn in 1975 with the opening of the Cleddau Bridge.

Powered by a compound diagonal engine, and with ornate brasswork and beautifully decorated paddle boxes, the handsome little steamer slipped into the water from the yard of Isaac J. Abdela & Mitchell Ltd at Queensferry, a yard better known for building barges. While externally she was an attractive vessel, inside, her passenger accommodation was, for a river ferry, reported to have been typically basic.

She had a crew of four, was licensed to carry 216 passengers, and could accommodate up to five vehicles on the forward deck.

On the official 1926 Mercantile Navy List she was recorded as vessel No.137061. According to that list – which identified her as SS *Menna* – she was then owned by the 'Mayor, Alderman & Burgesses of the Borough of Caernarvon, manager Edward Hall'. Being less than 100grt, she was not included on Lloyd's Registry.

Below: Offering a direct comparison with the plans, *opposite*, a profile view of the ferry under way, 23 September 1949. In this view the hull plating around the car deck between bows and paddle box has been replaced with railings, possibly to speed up the loading and unloading of the growing number of cars using the service.

PS *Alumchine* making her way across the River Cleddau, in an undated photograph. The style of the passengers' clothing would suggest that this view dates from the mid-to-late 1950s.

The yard in which *Menna* was built had opened in the 1880s as Smith & Company. Less than a decade later, having been known briefly as J. Wilson and Company, the site was occupied by the Queensferry Shipbuilding and Engineering Company, but even they were short-lived.

The yard was reopened in 1908 by Isaac J. Abdela & Mitchell Ltd, but they survived only until 1925, so the 76grt vessel – which was to have been named PS *Menai* – was one of their last contracts.

Her Menai Straits career was brief, and by 1929 she had been registered in London to the James Dredging, Towage & Transport Company Ltd. Sold on again in 1933 – by which time she was known as PS *Alumchine* – she was moved to south-west Wales where she operated the ferry service between Hobb's Point in Pembroke Dock and Neyland on behalf of the County Council.

Initially she was operated on behalf of the council by Frederick R. Lees of Pembroke Dock – who described himself as 'Managing Owner' – but the vessel was sold in 1945 to British Conveyances Ltd, and finally to Pembrokeshire Council in 1948, along with the Clyde-built screw steamer, SS *Lady Magdalen*, launched in 1896 by Russell & Company of Port Glasgow as the ferry SS *Clutha 11*.

With the introduction in 1956 of the larger capacity but much more utilitarian PS *Cleddau Queen* – the last paddle ferry built in Britain and built locally at Pembroke Dock – *Alumchine* became the reserve vessel until finally withdrawn in 1962.

In early June 1962, the Paddle Steamer Preservation Society was showing interest in saving the ferry. W. R. Horwood, the Honorary Secretary of the London & Home Counties Branch noted in a letter to Alex Esplen & Company that "The next ten years will, we feel sure, see the demise of the last British paddle vessel, and we are keen to acquire as much information as we can about those remaining, the which the above is the smallest." Esplens had been the consulting engineers appointed by Caernarfon Council to oversee the vessel's construction.

Even in 1962, confusion existed over her name, with Horwood identifying her as "PS *Menai, Menna* or *Menat*" in his letters to J. Shirley Esplen.

In the Spring 1963 issue of *Paddle Wheels*, the journal of the PSPS, the Society proudly announced that despite having been in existence for only three years, it had achieved one of its primary goals – the acquisition of its first paddle steamer. PS *Almunchine,* had been laid up on the Neyland slipway for just a few months when the PSPS offered to buy her for just £806. It seemed that her future was assured. All that was still needed was funding to move her from Neyland. That funding never materialised and the dream was short-lived – although it was 'technical problems' which were cited for the project's collapse – the ferry being sent to the breakers later that year. Four years later, the PSPS achieved its dream with the purchase of PS *Kingswear Castle,* and the rest, as they say, is history.

The opportunity to rescue and restore a working paddle ferry rather than an excursion boat never arose again, and today all that survives of PS *Menna/Alumchine* is a plan drawing, a few photographs, and Mrs Richards' mis-named silver plaque.

The Paddle Steamer Preservation Society, however, goes from strength to strength. To join and help preserve Britain's paddle steamer heritage, go to:

www.paddlesteamers.org.uk/join.htm

PS *Alumchine* after she was withdrawn from service, boarded up, without her mast, and abandoned at Neyland in 1962.

A DREAM TOO FAR

IT SHOULD HAVE BEEN a momentous occasion on 3 November 1857, with a crowd of many thousands watching, and a photographer lined up to take an historic picture as the biggest ship in the world slid sideways into the River Thames.

At 12:30 pm Henrietta Hope, the daughter of one of the major investors in the vessel, christened her *Leviathan* much to the surprise of everyone – including Brunel – as it had been widely expected that she would be named *Great Eastern*. Indeed her name was eventually changed to *Great Eastern* in July 1858.

But it was not just her naming which failed to go according to expectations. The great ship refused to move more than a few feet – the stern moved four, the bows three – and despite a complex system of steam winches and hydraulic rams, *Leviathan* thereafter stayed firmly rooted to her slipway. And to make matters worse, a labourer lost his life when crushed by one of the steam winches designed to help move the vessel towards the water.

To take the photographs, which they planned to use as the basis for engravings, *The Illustrated Times* had commissioned 25 year old Robert Howlett, then a rising star in the world of photography. He may not have been able to photograph the launch, but the series of large-format pictures which he took

Opposite. Brunel's SS *Great Eastern* takes shape on the stocks at the David Napier yard on the Isle of Dogs. The yard had been leased by J. Scott Russell & Co. whose own adjacent yard at Millwall was too small to accommodate the vessel. Photographed by Robert Howlett on 2 November 1857, the launch had been scheduled for the following day.

Below: The *Great Eastern* off Southampton, an early 1860s stereocard by George Washington Wilson of Aberdeen.

Top: An 1858 booklet about the SS *Great Eastern* "which will sail next spring".

Above: In the 1850s, nobody expected a steamship to depend on steam alone. This July 1853 advertisement for steamer sailings in the *North British Advertiser* used a little graphic which showed both paddles and sails.

survive as a testament to the vision of her designer, Isambard Kingdom Brunel.

At 18,915grt and nearly seven hundred feet long, she was not just the biggest ship ever built, she was several times larger than any other vessel ever to have been launched.

Robert Howlett exhibited his views of the great ship at the Exhibition of the Photographic Society in February-March 1858, just a few weeks after *Leviathan* was eventually floated on 31 January 1858. One of those exhibited was titled simply 'Portrait of I.K.Brunel Esq.' – the portrait which has become one of photography's iconic images – usually known as 'Isambard Kingdom Brunel standing before the chains of the *Great Eastern*', but of course that was not the name with which she had been christened.

The launch chains had been intended to slow down the vessel's journey towards the river, but on November 3 they remained fully wound on their huge wooden drums, their role postponed for another day.

In addition to the Brunel portrait, Howlett included in the exhibition six other studies of *Leviathan* taken both on board, and in and around the shipyard, with a seventh taken from across the river at Deptford.

Working with fellow photographer George Downes throughout 1857, Howlett also produced a remarkable series of 3D stereoscopic views of the ship under construction, today highly prized by photographic collectors. Whether or not he undertook any additional photography on the vessel during 1858 is not recorded, and by 2 December, having succumbed to typhus fever, he was dead at the age of 27.

The ship was originally intended to be built at the yard of John Scott Russell & Company at Millwall – who had leased the failing Fairbairn yard at Millwall Iron Works in 1848 – but it was quickly realised that the yard would never be able to accommodate a ship of such a size.

Russell elected to lease the nearby Napier Yard, but that decision, and Napier's location on the river would impact on just about every aspect of the ship's construction.

Left: The *Great Eastern* at her New York berth on the Hudson River in 1860, from a stereoscopic card by George Stacy. This photograph probably marks her debut at New York on 28 June 1860. Well known for his extensive catalogue of New York river scenes, Stacy's studio and printing factory were based in Rockland County, New York State.

Below: Robert Howlett's famous picture of Brunel was reproduced widely. Most popular, however, was the small *carte-de-visite* card-mounted version, published in 1858 by the London Stereoscopic Company.

Everything about the ship stretched engineering know-how to its limits. Too big to be launched stern first into the narrow river, Brunel and Russell had to devise and construct a special launch ramp to allow the ship to slip into the river sideways, but due to some errors in the construction of that ramp – too gentle a slope, and a slight rise towards the middle of its length – together with the sheer deadweight of the vessel itself, the crowd on 3 November 1857 went away disappointed.

Parts of the construction ramp have been uncovered and preserved on the Thames shore at Millwall, where remains of the slipway can also be seen.

The failed launch was just one in a series of problems which had beset Brunel's grandest – and final – project. Her keel had been laid on 1 May 1854, with a scheduled construction time of three and a

Right: Brunel's
SS *Great Britain* had
originally been
designed as a paddle
steamer, but during
construction he was
persuaded that a
screw propeller
would work better.
Thomas Guppy's huge
engines were simply
turned through 90°
and fitted with a
chain drive on to the
propeller shaft.
Illustrated are the
replica engines fitted
to the restored
SS *Great Britain* now
back in the Bristol
drydock in which she
was originally built.

Right: A remarkably
well-preserved
section of what is
believed to have
been the SS *Great
Eastern's* wooden
launch ramp was
uncovered during
redevelopment of
the Millwall riverside.

Left: At low tide, parts of the stone and concrete base of the slipway can still be seen at the river's edge.

THE
GREAT EASTERN
(launched 1858)
largest steamship
of the century
was built here by
I.K.Brunel and
J.Scott Russell

Top: a blue plaque above an archway next to the former J. Scott Russell offices on Westferry Road *(above)* commemorates the role of both Brunel and Russell in the building of the ship, despite Russell's bankruptcy two years into the project.

Above left: The former 'Plate House' building in the Russell yard is where much of the ship's ironwork was formed.

half years, but by early in 1856, Russell's company was in dire financial difficulties, and to save the project from collapse, a consortium including the Eastern Steam Navigation Company had to take over the management of the project.

According to folklore, it is said that during her construction, two riveters mysteriously vanished, and stories persisted that they had been sealed into the ship's revolutionary double-skinned hull!

The *Great Eastern* was very much a hybrid, driven by both a propeller and paddle wheels, together with an estimated 58,000 sq.ft. of canvas hung from six masts. Large steam engines by Russell amidships drove the 56ft diameter paddle wheels, while another, by James Watt & Co., positioned

23

Opposite top: The SS *Great Eastern* at sea, probably 1860. It is interesting to note than in none of the engravings or lithographs is the ship's livery the same as seen in George Stacy's 1860 photographs.

Right: A contemporary engraving of the SS *Great Eastern* at her moorings after her eventual launch on 31 January 1858.

Middle: A stereoscopic view of passengers — or perhaps sightseers — on board the SS *Great Eastern*, 1860. Believed to have been taken in New York harbour by George Stacy.

Right: SS *Great Eastern* arriving in New York Harbour on June 28 1860, engraved from a view sketched by an artist working for *Harper's Weekly*.

further aft, powered the 24ft four-blade screw. To raise steam for them required ten massive boilers, and to fuel their furnaces, she carried 12,000 tons of coal.

Twenty years before the SS *Great Eastern* had even entered the water, the design for Brunel's pioneering iron-hulled SS *Great Britain* – herself originally conceived as a paddler – had been changed to accommodate a propeller, Thomas Guppy's enormous engine being turned through 90° to drive a propeller shaft rather than two paddle wheels.

At 3,650grt, the SS *Great Britain* was a mere fraction of the size of *Great Eastern*, and for the very much larger ship Brunel had believed that, to ensure both her continuous operation and smoother passage, the combination of screw, paddles and sails would prove to be a more reliable solution. Having made that decision – and recognising the requirement that the propeller must be able to act independently of the

Above: A handy guide – for the anticipated crowds of visitors – detailing the SS *Great Eastern's* statistics, was produced to coincide with her first visit to New York in 1860.

Below: A mid-1860s woodcut of SS *Great Eastern* during her years as a cable-laying ship.

paddles – balancing the output of the separate engines once the vessel was underway cannot have been easy.

Thus, she was originally built with five tall funnels, but despite several contemporary illustrations showing her underway, smoke streaming from all five, and a massive area of sail deployed, that was never the case. It was found that sails could not be used in conjunction with the paddles or screw, except on the first two masts as the exhaust from the boiler furnaces would have set them alight!

Brunel's vision had been for a ship which could sail to Australia and back without refuelling – coal had yet to be discovered in Australia – and he believed that there were significant economies of scale if he built a ship capable of carrying the same passenger load as several smaller ones. In that respect, he was quickly proved wrong – or simply ahead of his time – and as a passenger ship she was a commercial failure, but he would not live to learn that, dying on 15 September 1859 at the age of just 53. He had collapsed with a stroke on board *Great Eastern* on 9 September, and it is said that being told a few days later of an explosion on board during her sea trials – which killed a number of the ship's crew – was what finally caused his demise.

His dream of a triumphant entrance into New York harbour on board the biggest ship in the world, and the engineering marvel of the day, would never be realised.

On her maiden voyage to America, fewer than 200 of her 4,000 passenger berths had been taken up, and even on her most successful Atlantic crossing, she was only a little over half full. Achieving the economics of scale which Brunel had envisaged were, of course, only possible if she was substantially full. As a temporary tourist attraction in New York harbour, she attracted many times the number of people who had travelled on her. And that statistic was repeated wherever she went

Although she enjoyed a short and unsuccessful life as a passenger liner, *Great Eastern* was a significant technical achievement, and she is remembered as the largest paddle steamer ever constructed – by some considerable measure. Brunel's vision of huge passenger liners was simply half a century ahead of its time.

Had there been no further use for her, *Great Eastern* might have been scrapped after just a few years but her size, her massive carrying capacity, and her motive power combined to make her ideal for an important international role.

Using both propeller and paddle drive, she was a very stable ship, and with her revolutionary double hull, a very safe one. Indeed during her life she survived a greater tear in her hull plating than that which would sink the *Titanic* almost half a century later.

But it was her sheer size which made her an obvious choice to undergo conversion for use as a cable-laying ship. With funnel No.4 and two of her boilers removed, her passenger accommodation stripped out and replaced by three huge 'cable tanks', the heavily modified ship, after several serious mishaps, eventually successfully laid the second transatlantic telegraph cable in 1865-6, and several other cables thereafter.

No other ship in the world had the capacity to carry the 2,600 mile long cable. She had finally found a role which she could undertake profitably, and was used to lay cables across the Indian Ocean as well as the Atlantic.

After her cable-laying duties came to an end, the ship was sold to an entrepreneur who planned to refit her and operate

Below: A colour lithograph printed c.1865, French maritime artist Louis le Breton (1818-1866) offered a very inaccurate profile of the SS *Great Eastern* with oddly-shaped paddle boxes and short stubby funnels. The positions of the funnels are also wrong, as funnel 3 was closer to the mainmast, and there was a gap behind it where funnel 4 had been before it was removed during her conversion into a cable-laying ship. The rear funnel in the re-configured vessel was further aft, and closer to mast 5.

Her last voyage – a contemporary woodcut of the steamship as she is towed to her final destination off Rock Ferry on the Mersey.

her as a liner once more, but profits again proved elusive, and by the early 1880s, it was clear her useful days were effectively over.

In 1885, she was leased to the owner of Lewis's department store in Liverpool, and moored in the Mersey with an advertisement for the shop painted along her side, and an exhibition in the main public areas – a somewhat ignominious end for such a revolutionary ship. Lewis's also had stores in Dublin and Glasgow at that time, so the SS *Great Eastern* also did tours of duty off both those ports, but by 1888 her fate was sealed. As *The New York Times* reported on 8 September 1888, under the headline '*Great Eastern* Beached' – picking up a report from *The Times* in London

The steamship Great Eastern, *which has passed through so many vicissitudes since her launch 30 years ago, was successfully beached near New-Ferry on the Cheshire shore of the Mersey on Saturday. Since last December, when she became the property of Messrs. Henry Bath & Co. of Liverpool, the Great Eastern had been moored in the Clyde between Helensburg [sic!] and Greenock, and in the inspection which she has undergone, unexpected value is said to have been discovered. Last Wednesday at noon she was got under way, and started on what is intended to be her last voyage. With her own steam she could make a speed of four to five knots, but she was towed by the powerful steam tug* Stormcock. *The weather was bright when the vessel started, but next morning the wind freshened, while dark masses of clouds presaged thr presaged the dirty weather that followed.*

The storm they met off the Isle of Man meant that the tug had to cast the big vessel adrift for a time, but as the gales abated, the hawser was reconnected and she continued her journey towards the Mersey. After an account of her travails en route, the report ended in a somewhat more positive vein than might have been expected, offering a glimmer of hope

The Great Eastern *now lies about 200 yards to the southward of the New-Ferry stage. It is said that the ship will now be broken up and the material sold, but there are persons who believe that*

Moored on the
Mersey in September
1888 — one of the
last photographs of
the SS *Great Eastern*
before she was
broken up,
photographed for the
Dundee photographic
publisher James
Valentine.

some use will yet be found for the vessel designed by Brunel.

It was a false hope, and the biggest paddle-steamer ever built was eventually broken up on the beach at Rock Ferry, where, a century and a quarter later, fragments of her hull plating and rivets are still periodically revealed after heavy tides. Her mainmast was, of course, saved and still stands at the Kop-end of Liverpool FC's Anfield stadium. So strongly was she built, that it took 200 men nearly two years to break her up. Long before her demise, screw-driven steamers had proved their worth both in terms of ease of steering, and ability to cope with heavy seas. And at higher speeds their smooth motion was much more comfortable for their passengers.

It would be nearly fifty years before anyone attempted to design a ship as large as her again, by which time paddles would not even enter their thinking. White Star Line's RMS *Oceanic* launched in 1899 was four feet longer and SS *Celtic*, completed for White Star in 1901, at 20,904grt, had a greater displacement

Paddle steamers would, however, continue to be built in large numbers in British yards until the outbreak of the Second World War, but they were all pleasure steamers.

A few more were constructed in the post-war years – most notably PS *Waverley* – and the last large paddler to come off the stocks in a British yard would be the Loch Lomond pleasure steamer PS *Maid of the Loch*, 95 years after the launch of the *Great Eastern*. Efforts to return *Maid of the Loch* to steam are detailed elsewhere in this book and will continue for several years yet.

A LITTLE HISTORY

O N THE EDGE of a supermarket car park in Port Glasgow, behind an unnecessarily heavy black iron fence whose bars are just a little too close together for a camera to be pushed through them, stands a strange-looking craft. This is the paddle steamer *Comet* – or at least a replica of her – the first-ever passenger-carrying paddle steamer in Britain, and the first example of a vessel for which the shipyards on the Clyde went on to became world-famous.

As with every 'first', there are competing claims, and while *Comet* was certainly not the first viable steamboat, she was certainly the first in Britain to successfully carry fare-paying passengers.

She was not the world's first passenger boat either, however, as across the Atlantic, John Fitch had successfully operated a steamboat on the Delaware River in 1786. In the same year, the state of New Jersey granted him exclusive rights to operate steamers on the river, and he inaugurated a passenger-carrying service between Philadelphia and New Jersey as early as the summer of 1790.

Fitch's early creations, however, were a far cry from the steamers with which the world would later become familiar.

Using a modified Newcomen engine, his *Perseverance* of 1787 used steam-powered oars along either side of the vessel, while his successful 1790 passenger boat used

Opposite: *Comet's* iron paddles were simple, but inefficient. Two pairs on each side drove the ship, producing a smoother motion than single paddles of such basic design could have achieved.

Above: The replica Comet built in 1962.

Left: The origin of this carved stone – of which only the bottom half has survived – showing tradesmen and tools involved in the construction of Henry Bell's *Comet* in 1812 is unspecified, but it is thought to have come from a Victorian building in the town.

31

Right: A detailed model of Jouffrey's 1783 *Pyroscaphe* is in the Musée de la Marine, Paris.

steam-driven oars at the stern, creating a motion which has been likened to the feet-action of a swimming duck! For later steamboat designs, he experimented with paddle wheels, and even an early propeller.

Despite his perseverance, he was unsuccessful in persuading backers that steam propulsion had any future, and in 1793, he was similarly unsuccessful in persuading anyone to support his ambitions financially in France.

Timing, of course, is everything, and France in the 1790s was in the throes of the Reign of Terror as the Jacobins and Girondins fought for control of the country, and effectively turned the populace's attention elsewhere for some years.

Several others in France and Scotland claimed to have built the first steamboat – the strongest being that of Claude-François-Dorothée, marquis de Jouffrey d'Abbans (1751–1832), who successfully demonstrated a steamer on the River Saône near Lyons in 1783.

Below: Robert Fulton's paddle steamer designs featured on US stamps, in 1909 and 1965.

Jouffrey's steamboat, the *Pyroscaphe* – with primitive versions of the side paddles which would become so very familiar – used a steam engine converted from a pump which had been built for the French fire service.

The marquis got little credit for his invention – indeed he was forbidden from demonstrating it on the Seine in Paris – and the French Revolution of 1789 did the same for him as it would for Fitch a few years later.

It would be many years before his powerful claim to have invented the paddle steamer was recognised, first by Arago, and in 1840 by the French Academie des sciences.

Long before that, however, the American inventor Robert Fulton had demonstrated his steamboat on the Seine in 1803. His interest in steamboats was a far cry from his early apprenticeship as a jeweller, and later profession as a landscape and portrait painter. He had arrived in Britain in 1787, and became acquainted with James Watt, who had sparked his interest in engineering in general, and steam power in particular. Some usually-reliable sources even point to him having had contact with, and support from, Henry Bell who would later commission *Comet*, but that remains no more than conjecture.

Early work on canal design led Fulton to a 1794 patent for the use of 'inclined planes' as an alternative to canal locks, but, after he moved to Paris in the later 1790s, he became interested in naval warfare, and pioneered an early design for a submarine before his 1803 experiment with steam propulsion.

Returning to America, four years later in 1807, and under the patronage of the American politician and ambassador to France, Richard Livingston, he introduced the first commercial steamer, the *North River Steamboat* – its name was reportedly later changed to *Clermont* when she was substantially rebuilt and enlarged between 1808 and 1809. The vessel carried its first passengers between New York and Albany, covering the 150 miles between the two cities at a reported speed of more than twelve miles per hour. Drawing on his contacts in England, *Clermont* was powered by an early steam engine manufactured by Boulton & Watt of Birmingham.

In 1808, in the state legislature, he acquired monopoly rights to operate steam ships on the Hudson River. That act gave Fulton, Livingston and their associates exclusive rights, depending on the total number of steamers built, to commission and run steamers on the river for up to 30 years.

To commemorate three hundred years since the 'discovery' of the Hudson River in 1609, and, belatedly, to mark the centenary of Fulton's first passenger-carrying steamer, a replica of the *North River Steamboat*, named *Clermont* was built in 1909. The 1807 vessel was a larger and clearly more sophisticated ship than the *Comet* introduced on to the Clyde three years later. Here the replica boat is seen on the river, *bottom*, and tied up during the Hudson-Fulton commemorative celebrations, *below*. Intriguingly, some of the contemporary paintings of the original ship show her paddles concealed in paddle boxes. The replica was broken up in 1936.

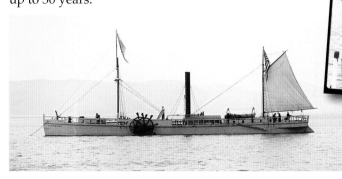

In a career which spanned many aspects of engineering, Fulton is also remembered for designing the world's first steam-powered warship – which he intended to name *Demologos* – for the US Navy in 1812. He died before she was completed, and the warship was eventually named *Fulton* in his honour. A novel twin-hulled design, her single paddle-wheel was positioned between the two hulls.

Top: A Will's cigarette card produced in 1911 showing the stern-wheeled *Charlotte Dundas* underway in 1803. It is unlikely that she ever encountered such choppy conditions on the Forth and Clyde Canal.

Below: The 3/4 size replica hull of the *Charlotte Dundas*, built in 1988 by the Cockenzie Boatyard & Slipway Co., was displayed for a time at Falkirk Wheel. She is now in an Arbroath boatyard, her future uncertain.

The *Comet* which is on display in Port Glasgow today was built in 1962 to commemorate the 150th anniversary of the date in 1812 when the original *Comet* entered passenger service between Glasgow and Helensburgh.

The replica was built as a working vessel, complete with functioning steam engine, and fifty years ago she was filmed in several locations along the Clyde with smoke billowing from her tall funnel – what looks like her mast is, in fact, the funnel. But decades of neglect have subsequently reduced her to a static exhibit, which meant, of course, that she was not able to sail in 2012 to commemorate the 200th anniversary of her introduction into service.

Comet was built for Henry Bell, a former stonemason who had worked with the great engineer John Rennie. Bell and his wife had moved to Helensburgh, he as superintendent of the town's baths, and she to run their hotel. He was fascinated by the idea of steam power, and was already aware of the experimental stern-wheeler *Charlotte Dundas* which had steamed along a length of the Forth and Clyde Canal near Glasgow as early as 1803.

Charlotte Dundas was the brain-child of William Symington who, sponsored by Lord Dundas, had recognised the commercial value of James Watt's steam engines. Built by John Allen, and powered by a simple steam engine manufactured at the Carron Foundry near Falkirk, the little vessel, with Dundas on board, made her first voyage in

The 1823 engine from the PS *Leven*, built by Robert Napier at Camlachie near Govan. The cast-iron engine was built by Napier's manager and designer David Elder, and fitted into PS *Leven* – built by James Lang of Dumbarton for the Dumbarton Steamboat Company. *Leven* was broken up in 1841, and her engine was subsequently fitted into PS *Queen of Beauty* – built at Napier's own yard at Lancefield – where it operated for a further 22 years.

early January 1803. Her trial steamings were successful – she could tow barges carrying over seventy tons of freight – but it seems that fear that her wash would erode the canal banks caused the canal company to abandon the project.

Henry Bell hit saw the potential of a steamer service for bringing visitors to Helensburgh – and his wife's boarding-house, no doubt – from Glasgow, but it took over a decade for his original idea to reach fruition. In that time, the accolade of becoming the operator of the world's first passenger steamer had been claimed by in 1807 on the other side of the Atlantic.

Five years later, Bell's *Comet*, built for him by John Wood of Port Glasgow, became Britain's first passenger-carrying steamer.

Her paddles were very basic and rather inefficient, but still she proved a very popular vessel for the few years she was in service. But, as with any 'first', others learned from Bell's design – and its shortcomings – and quickly evolved larger and more efficient craft.

In 1823, in Glasgow, Robert Napier was awarded the contract to build the engine for the paddle steamer *Leven*, and his side-lever engine still survives, now on permanent display outside the Denny Ship Model Experiment Tank in

Below: HMS *Terrible* was built at Deptford and launched in 1845. Her engines, manufactured by Maudslay, Sons & Field of Lambeth, gave her a top speed of over 10 knots. At the time of her launch, she was the largest wooden-hulled steam frigate in the Royal Navy, and served until 1879. In 1854, HMS *Terrible* took part in the siege of Sevastopol during the Crimean War. This illustration is from an edition of prints produced by the London-born engraver Henry Papprill, published by Ackermann, and based on a painting by British artist William Adolphus Knell.

Dumbarton. It powered the PS *Leven* for seventeen years before being installed in the PS *Queen of Beauty* in 1845, where it worked until 1863. This is believed to have been Napier's first marine engine, and thus of great historic importance – a fact not lost on his family who, in 1877, presented it to the town of Dumbarton. Of the PS *Leven* herself, little is known except that she regularly sailed between Dumbarton and Glasgow, and in the summer operated excursions down the west coast of Scotland and around Ailsa Craig. Napier's subsequent engines would power many of the finest 19th century Clyde-built ships.

To a world which had never previously seen a steamer, these new craft, belching smoke and with no sails in evidence, were initially a source of surprise and sometimes even fear.

Three years after the launch of PS *Leven*, in August 1826, the *Inverness Courier* newspaper carried an account of the first passenger steamship to sail round the north of Scotland. The PS *United Kingdom* sailed from Glasgow, through the Hebrides, round Cape Wrath, up to Orkney, south again to Wick, Aberdeen and Newhaven on the Firth of Forth. Several sightings of early steamships belching smoke as they made their way slowly along the north west coast of Scotland at the time were reported as being 'ships on fire'.

Despite their vessels being small – and the seas sometimes very rough – shipping companies very quickly recognised the speed advantage of steam over sail, and initiated what must have seemed very high speed passenger services. One of the earliest services between London and the North of Scotland – a distance of seven hundred miles – was operated by the Aberdeen Steam Navigation Company, who introduced passenger and freight sailings between Aberdeen and London as early as 1828, just fifteen years after the first sailing of Bell's *Comet*. Their steamers completed the journey in a fraction of the time previously taken by sailing ships, opening up the possibility of fresh fish landed at Aberdeen, and locally manufactured goods, being on sale in London just a day later. In the days long before there were railway links between the two cities, paddle steamers opened up completely new commercial markets.

The speed of development of paddle steamers throughout the next three decades was remarkable. Just twenty-five years after *Comet* first sailed, Brunel's 1700grt PS *Great Western* was launched, and only five years after that, the Royal Navy was ordering wooden-hulled paddle frigates – such as the huge and heavily-armed HMS *Terrible* – which boasted a displacement of over 3,000 tons.

Paddle steamers and screw steamers in Balaklava harbour, 8 March 1855, during the Crimean War. The shape and ornamentation on the paddle boxes suggests that the paddle steamer in the centre of the picture may be HMS *Hecla*, a 4-gun Hydra class sloop, built at Chatham Dockyard in 1839 and driven by a side lever steam engine from Scott & Sinclair of Greenock. This was the vessel on which Victorian photographer Roger Fenton – who took this picture – sailed from Britain to the Crimea at the beginning of his expedition to the seat of the war.

Right: The great storm at Balaklava about which Simpson wrote, was eventually reported in the British media some time after the event – it took several days for news to get home – and *The Illustrated London News* commissioned this woodcut of both paddle steamers and screw-driven vessels being overwhelmed by the reportedly ferocious seas.

The engines for both those vessels came from the Lambeth engineering firm of Maudslay, Sons & Field, one of the leading manufacturers of railway locomotives, pumping engines and marine steam engines at the time.

When Britain went to war in the Crimea in 1854, in addition to traditional sailing ships and a number of screw-driven steamers, the Royal Navy still operated a considerable number of small wooden-hulled paddle-driven sloops.

One of them, HMS *Hecla*, regularly steamed from the Thames to Balaclava, carrying men and much needed supplies. Almost lost in a storm off Gibraltar in January 1855 when her masts had to be cut away to avoid her being overturned by the stormy waters, the little vessel managed to make port by steam power alone – although *The Illustrated London News* subsequently published a story and an engraving about her 'loss at sea'.

Right: Lying on the seabed off Lundy, the skeletal remains of the hull of PS *Iona* (II).

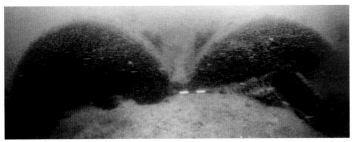

Left: Two of the boilers of PS *Iona* (II). They raised steam for Thomson's powerful and efficient two-cylinder oscillating engine. The voyage was shrouded in secrecy, her true destination not revealed. Indeed her route was listed as being from the Clyde bound for Nassau. Her loss was announced in *The Commercial Daily List* on February 4 1864, which also reported that her crew had all been rescued.

Repaired, re-masted, and back in service just a month later, she transported the pioneer war photographer Roger Fenton with his assistants, a horse-drawn darkroom and all the paraphernalia of Victorian photography to Balaklava, arriving there on 8 March.

The supplies HMS *Hecla* was carrying were, in part, to replace equipment lost in a storm which had struck the Crimean peninsula in November 1854 – and which had exposed the vulnerability of paddle steamers under such conditions. The war artist William Simpson, whose lithographic prints are now an important part of the war record, arrived in Balaklava on 16 November 1854, the day after the storm, and wrote vividly of what he found

Whichever way you looked, you saw paddle-boxes, bows, sterns, many funnels and gangways of the various injured vessels, floating about in the water. None seems to have escaped. Lord Cardigan's yacht had her gunwale smashed in. It is difficult to conceive how so much mischief could have occurred in such a snug little harbour; but it would seem the ships were all lying so close together that they ground one another to pieces. Eight ships are reported to have sunk here, and about four thousand men were drowned.

Records are scant, but at odds with Simpson's account, however, and some sources note that 34 ships were destroyed or severely damaged, at a cost of one thousand lives. A significant number of the vessels lost had, apparently, been paddle steamers. Lessons were not immediately learned from the incident, however, and Roger Fenton's photograph taken in March 1855 – *see page 37* – shows ships still being moored in such a way that their paddle boxes are butted up alongside those of the adjacent vessels.

THE ONCE-UBIQUITOUS PADDLE STEAMER

Cunard's PS *Britannia* arriving In Boston in winter, from a contemporary woodcut, late 1840s. Of the immediate effect of the stormy crossing on the little paddle steamer, Dickens, *above*, wrote that he was awakened in his cabin one morning by his wife's screams, and saw that "The water-jug is plunging and leaping like a lively dolphin; all the smaller articles are afloat, except my shoes, which are stranded on a carpet-bag, high and dry, like a couple of coal-barges. Suddenly I see them spring into the air, and behold the looking-glass, which is nailed to the wall, sticking fast upon the ceiling. At the same time the door entirely disappears, and a new one is opened in the floor. Then I begin to comprehend that the state-room is standing on its head. Before it is possible to make any arrangement at all compatible with this novel state of things, the ship rights."

By the end of the 1850s, nearly all new naval ships were screw-propelled, but large passenger-carrying paddle steamers would continue to be built for decades to come. Indeed, despite the conditions they had to cope with, transatlantic paddle steamers, first introduced in the late 1830s, continued to be operated for nearly forty years before finally giving way to large screw vessels.

In these days of huge transatlantic liners, it is easy to forget just how small some of the vessels were which made the crossing to America. More than a few did not make it.

One notable 'failure' was never designed for transatlantic service. She was the second paddle steamer to be named *Iona*, built by J. & G. Thomson in 1863 for David Hutcheson's services to Scotland's Western Isles. The 368grt steamer, with a draught of only nine feet, was equipped with a two-cylinder oscillating engine which could drive her at 18 knots. Some accounts suggested she could reach 24 knots, but it is highly unlikely that she could achieve such a speed.

After just a few weeks in service she was sold to a representative of the Confederate States, for use as a blockade-runner during the American Civil War. Her purchaser was Charles Hopkins Bostier of Richmond, Virginia, and she sailed for America in January 1864. Not surprisingly, after getting caught in bad weather on her voyage south from the Clyde, her crew came close to mutiny, worried about her ability to cope with the Atlantic conditions. The steamer had, after all, only been built to deal with the sort of weather conditions she would encounter around the Scottish islands. She was never built to face heavy Atlantic waves, nor did she

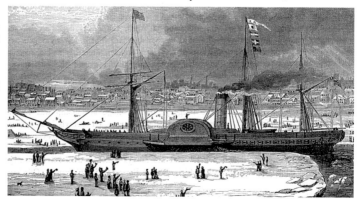

The Peninsular & Orient Steam Navigation Company's 2082grt SS *Nyanza* was built at the Blackwall yard of the Thames Ironworks and Shipbuilding Company and delivered to P&O at the end of 1864. She was powered by oscillating steam engines built by J. & G. Rennie of Millwall with a theoretical 2304ihp, delivering a maximum speed of 12 knots. She was designed to carry 143 first class passengers, with just 34 in second class, on the company's services between Southampton and Alexandria in Egypt. She was sold in 1873 to the Union Steamship Company of Southampton who lengthened her, and fitted a 2-cylinder compound engine by Gourlay of Dundee, driving a propellor.

ever do so, sinking off the east coast of Lundy in the Bristol Channel on 2 February 1864.

The wreck was located quickly and salvaged, many of the fittings recovered being used in her replacement, PS *Iona* (III) which sailed for over 70 years. How she might have fared across the Atlantic, nobody knows. The vessel's exact location on the seabed was rediscovered during an archaeological dive, during which many still-recognisable features of the vessel were logged and photographed.

The brief era of the trans-Atlantic paddler was dominated by just a few shipping lines, probably the best known of which grew out of the Glasgow steamship operators George and James Burns who, after selling their Scottish coastal steamers to David Hutcheson, went into partnership with the Canadian Samuel Cunard.

The Cunard Line – originally known as the British & North American Steamship Company – operated regular fortnightly sailings to Halifax, Nova Scotia, and to Boston, from 1840, using the specially constructed, wooden-hulled, 1150grt paddle steamers *Britannia, Acadia* and *Caledonia,* built by three Clyde yards – Robert Duncan & Company, John & Charles Wood, and Robert Steele & Company, sub-contracted from Robert Napier who constructed the two-cylinder side-lever engines.

A sister ship, PS *Columbia,* joined the fleet in 1841, and two larger vessels, PS *Hibernia* and PS *Cambria,* at 1400grt each, were added in 1843 and 1845 respectively, *Hibernia* initiating services to New York. *Columbia* was wrecked off Halifax Nova Scotia in 1843, her eighty-five passengers and crew being rescued without loss.

Top: The 1840-built SS *President* seen in a contemporary aquatint. At 2360grt and 243 feet in length, she was the largest and fastest steamship of her day, powered by 540nhp engines built by Fawcett, Preston & Company at their Phoenix Foundry in York Street, Liverpool. Fawcett, Preston & Co. had built their first marine steam engine as early as 1817 — for the wooden-hulled Mersey ferry PS *Etna* which operated services between Liverpool and Tranmere.

Right: An illustration produced after the loss of the SS *President*. The caption claimed that "As last seen from the Packet Ship ORPHEUS Capt. COLE in the terrific gale of March the 12th 1841 at 5 o'clock P.M. Lat. 39, 46. Long. 71, bearing N.E. by E. by Compass steering East. In the inquiry before the British Consul, June the 5th 1841, Capt. Cole of the Packet Ship Orpheus, stated that when he last saw the President on the 12th of March she was rising on the top of a tremendous sea pitching heavily and laboring tremendously." An almost identical scene, of *President* surviving a previous storm, had however been published in 1840.

An early passenger on PS *Britannia* was Charles Dickens, whose description of a transatlantic crossing on such a fragile vessel, during which several lifeboats were lost overboard, and the paddle boxes were partly destroyed, makes alarming reading. Of his experience he wrote

I say nothing of what may be called the domestic noises of the ship, such as breaking glass and crockery, the tumbling down of stewards, the gambols, overhead, of loose casks and truant dozens of bottled porter, and the very remarkable and far from exhilarating sound made by seventy passengers too ill to get up to breakfast. I say nothing of them: for although I lay listening to this concert for three or four days, I don't think I

A contemporary engraving in *The Illustrated London News* showed SS *Bywell Castle* slicing PS *Princess Alice* in two. PS *Princess Alice* was, in fact, making her way across the river to calmer water when she was struck by the 904grt freighter, having changed her course just as the pilot on board *Bywell Castle* had taken what he believed would be effective evasive action.

heard it for more than a quarter of a minute, at the expiration of which term, I lay down again, excessively sea-sick.

On a voyage like that – and with roast pork and beer the only option he mentions on the menu – who could blame them! Dickens, however, used the experience to create a dramatic word picture in his book *American Notes*, published in 1850.

The labouring of the ship in the troubled sea on this night I shall never forget. 'Will it ever be worse than this?' was a question I had often heard asked, when everything was sliding and bumping about, and when it certainly did seem difficult to comprehend the possibility of anything afloat being more disturbed, without toppling over and going down. But what the agitation of a steam-vessel is, on a bad winter's night in the wild Atlantic, it is impossible for the most vivid imagination to conceive. To say that she is flung down on her side in the waves, with her masts dipping into them, and that, springing up again, she rolls over on the other side, until a heavy sea strikes her with the noise of a hundred great guns, and hurls her back – that she stops, and staggers, and shivers, as though stunned, and then, with a violent throbbing at her heart, darts onward like a monster goaded into madness, to be beaten down, and battered, and crushed, and leaped on by the angry sea – that thunder, lightning, hail, and rain, and wind, are all in fierce contention for the mastery – that every plank has its groan, every nail its shriek, and every drop of water in the great ocean its howling voice – is nothing.

Launched in 1870 at Pembroke Royal Dockyard, the 1856grt HMY *Osborne* was, at 250 feet in length, one of the largest and finest steam yachts afloat. She was designed by Sir Edward James Reed the eminent naval architect, author and politician, who was the Chief Designer for the Royal Navy from 1863 until 1870. *Osborne* was one of his last designs. After leaving naval service he became Liberal MP for Pembroke in 1874. HMY *Osborne* was decommissioned in 1908 and broken up shortly afterwards. She is seen here at at the opening of the Kiel Canal in 1895 with the Prince and Princess of Wales on board.

Despite the appalling experience which Dickens described, those early trans-Atlantic crossings experienced surprisingly few serious disasters.

The first, and worst, was the loss of the PS *President*, built on the Thames in 1840 by Curling, Young & Company at Limehouse for the London-based British and American Steam Navigation Company. She first sailed from Liverpool to New York on 17 August 1840, completing the crossing in seventeen days, but, leaving New York on 12 March 1841 on her third return crossing with 136 passengers and crew on board, she foundered without survivors somewhere between the Nantucket Shoal and St George's Bank off the coast of Massachusetts. Her loss bankrupted the company.

The era of the trans-Atlantic paddler was quickly overtaken by the advent of more stable screw-driven ships, leaving paddle steamers with their shallow draught to develop as ideal vessels for shorter sailings, and for use as ferries and excursion boats. In those roles, paddle steamers enjoyed a further century of success.

But even excursion boats suffered some horrendous losses. Britain's worst pleasure steamer disaster befell the PS *Princess Alice* (ex PS *Bute*) on the evening of 3 September 1878, while returning to London from a 'Moonlight Trip' to Gravesend.

The 171grt steamer, originally built for the Wemyss Bay Railway Company by Caird of Greenock in 1865, had been acquired by the London Steamboat Company in 1875, and was in her fourth season operating on the Thames. At just 220 feet in length, and a 20 foot beam, she was nonetheless licensed to carry more than 900 passengers – a figure unimaginable in today's safety-conscious world. That night there were an estimated 750 people on board.

Small steamers coming up river, invariably struggling against the strong currents, often changed direction while seeking out calmer waters – a practice which caused the deaths of more than 600 people on board *Princess Alice*. She was struck amidships by the coal freighter SS *Bywell Castle*, sailing downstream bound for Newcastle. and sank within four minutes. Despite passenger numbers being below her licensed maximum, the inquest concluded that she was carrying too many people, while a public enquiry concluded that there might be fewer accidents in the future 'if proper and stringent rules and regulation were laid down for all steam navigation on the River Thames'.

As more powerful engines were developed, steamers became larger, faster, and more reliable. By the middle of the 1870s there were excursion boats – and royal yachts – with gross tonnages far in excess of the little wooden-hulled steamer in which Charles Dickens had crossed the Atlantic just three decades earlier.

As the century drew to a close, a number of major players had emerged as the excursion steamer gained popularity. Amongst them in the South-east, the fleets operated by the General Steam Navigation Company, the Victoria Steamboat Association, the Coastal Development Company (operating under a variety of names including the famous Belle Steamers), and New Palace Steamers Ltd, a subsidiary of the

The Woolwich ferry PS *Duncan* was built in 1888 by R. & H. Green of Blackwall, and was powered by condensing engines by John Peen & Son of Greenwich. *Duncan* worked the route for 34 years until withdrawn in 1922. The second quartet of paddle steamers, introduced in 1923, were of a similar design but much larger. The last paddle ferry on the service was withdrawn in 1971.

Main picture: The Denny Ship Model Experiment Tank as it looks today, 140 years after it was first opened. In its final form, it was over 300ft long, and survives as the oldest ship model test tank in the world.

Above: A model of a 9-float featherable paddle wheel constructed in the 1920s, 0.5 metres in diameter, and used in the Denny Tank to gather data designed to improve paddle steamer efficiency.

Clyde shipbuilders Fairfields, all enjoyed periods of great success as demand for passenger capacity grew. On the South and South-west coasts, Cosens & Company of Weymouth, and P. &. A Campbell based in Bristol controlled a huge proportion of the market.

Around Scotland's coasts in the closing years of the 19th century – where many of the boats operated vital local ferry links year round as well as excursions in the summer – two companies dominated although there were still many smaller operators. The two giants were David MacBrayne, and the Caledonian Steam Packet Company who between them built and operated some of the largest and most luxuriously appointed paddle steamers of the period.

The engineering side of ship design and shipbuilding was, by the last quarter of the 19th century, becoming much more scientific in its approach than hitherto, and one of the yards at the forefront of that new approach to ship design was William Denny & Brothers of Dumbarton.

Impressed by the pioneering work of William Froude of Torquay who had built a small tank in 1870 in which to test the efficiency of ships' hulls, William Denny persuaded his directors that there was a potential commercial advantage in using such a tank to measure the resistance of a model hull as it slipped through the water, and directly apply the data thus accumulated to the construction of the full-size vessel. In that way he could calculate the smallest engine required to achieve design speed, and thus considerably reduce a vessel's operating costs. To achieve this, in 1873 he built a tank over 240ft long, 20 feet wide, several feet deep and containing 2,500 tons of water, along which model hulls could be drawn at a controlled speed and in a controlled environment, and their resistance measured.

The tank was also used to test the efficiency of paddle wheel designs, determining the optimum number of floats per paddle, and the effectiveness of their feathering mechanisms in different wave conditions and speeds.

The tank remained in use for over a century and is all that remains of the Denny Brothers' yard today.

Around North Wales and the North-west, and on the North-east coasts, demand never achieved anything like the level elsewhere, and the market remained in the hands of smaller local operators.

Many paddle steamers were requisitioned by the War Office after the outbreak of the First World War and converted for naval use. After the war, however, the excursion market continued to grow, and many of the largest and finest steamers were commissioned. They too were requisitioned when the Second World War started, many converted for minesweeping duties, and several lost as a result.

PS *Medway Queen*, currently undergoing a major rebuild, earned her place in wartime history with her seven heroic journeys to Dunkirk rescuing hundreds of soldiers from the besieged beaches.

In the 1930s, some companies experimented with diesel-electric paddle vessels – *Talisman* entered service in 1935, but diesel-electric paddle ferries had been introduced on the River

After her rebuild, PS *Medway Queen* was towed out of Bristol's Albion Drydock on 24 October 2013 by the Plymouth tug *Christine*. She spent a few days in Cumberland Basin – moored at the same quayside at which Brunel's SS *Great Britain* was first photographed in 1845 – waiting for good weather before starting her long journey under tow back to Gillingham where her rebuild continues. Her hull was built at Abel's shipyard. SS *Great Britain* can be seen in Great Western Dock behind her, below.

47

Above: The 489grt drive-through ferry DEPV *Farringford* seen here during her sea trials on the Clyde in 1948 before delivery to the south coast.

Below: The Inglis-built DEPV *Talisman* approaching Dunoon, 24 June 1966, her final operational season. As HMS *Aristocrat*, she served as an anti-aircraft vessel in the Thames during World War II, as well as seeing some active service off the Normandy coast, where she was credited with shooting down three enemy aircraft. After being restored to her pre-war condition, she returned to service on the Clyde in 1946. She was offered for sale by A. M. C. McGinnity & Partners, on behalf of the British Railways Board, in late 1966, but with no buyers, she was broken up at Dalmuir in the following year.

Forth crossing the year before. The biggest to operate in Britain, the 489grt DEPV *Farringford*, entered service to the Isle of Wight in 1947, and spent her last seven years on the Humber until withdrawn in 1981.

New steamers continued to be ordered after the war, including the most famous – PS *Waverley* launched in October 1946 – but in fewer numbers, and although new paddle vessels were built, pre-war experiments with diesel-electric propulsion had encouraged shipbuilders that there were considerable operational savings to be made in abandoning steam power on smaller ships.

The first diesel-electric passenger vessel in Britain, the screw-driven MV *Lochfyne*, had been built in 1931 by Denny Brothers of Dumbarton for David MacBrayne, and was their first ship which offered the option of bridge control of the

engines rather than the practice of relaying bridge controls to the engine room via the conventional ship's telegraph. Dennys developed the idea in the first two ferries they built for the River Forth crossing – DEPV *Queen Margaret* and DEPV *Robert the Bruce* in 1934. The 544grt DEPV *Talisman*, built by A. & J. Inglis in 1935 for the LNER, was the first excursion paddler thus powered, and but for the intervention of World War II, more might have followed.

The 277grt DEPV *Sir William Wallace* being fitted out at Denny Brothers' yard on the River Leven at Dumbarton in late 1955. She was the third largest diesel-electric paddle vessel ever built in Britain, and served the Queensferry Passage across the River Forth until the Forth Road Bridge opened in 1964. It was the last of the four DEPVs built by Dennys. Two 175hp Crossley diesels generated electricity for the electric motors which, geared down, rotated the paddles via a chain drive at 45rpm.

After the war, Dennys built three more diesel-electric paddlers – *Farringford* in 1948, followed by *Mary Queen of Scots* in 1949, and *Sir William Wallace*, launched in late 1955 and entering service early in 1956.

At 178 feet long, and 489grt, *Farringford* was built for British Railways' Southern Region service between Lymington and Yarmouth on the Isle of Wight, ending her working life in Sealink colours on the Humber crossing. Plans to sell her to Western Ferries for their Dunoon to Gourock service in 1981 never materialised, and she was broken up in 1984.

The last paddler to leave a British yard was the ferry PS *Cleddau Queen* which entered service between Pembroke Dock and Neyland, alongside PS *Alumchine* in late 1956. However, after only twelve years, even *Cleddau Queen* proved inefficient and uneconomic, and was rebuilt as a diesel-powered twin-screw vessel.

In 1984, the little steel-hulled 9grt PS *Monarch*, the brainchild of Brian Waters, entered the water, and after a chequered history and recent extensive restoration, she now sails out of Wareham. Will she turn out to have been the last new paddle steamer built in Britain?

The new hull for the 1938-built PS *Medway Queen* has been completed in Bristol and she is now back in Gillingham looking externally splendid while being internally fitted out, her rebuild continuing. But is she really a restoration, albeit on an unprecedented scale, or virtually a new paddle steamer?

Will there be more new-builds? When the idea of building a brand new steam locomotive was first talked about, those behind the project were considered by many to be little short of mad. But, years and a lot of money later, the A1 'Peppercorn' Pacific *Tornado* is complete and in steam, with other 'new builds' in progress, giving steam railway locomotion a bright 21st century future.

On a maritime front, with talk of a replica *Titanic* perhaps being commercially viable, why not a replica *Jeanie Deans*? Perhaps in better economic times, someone might consider such a project.

Above: PS *Waverley* on one of her regular summer tours of Britain's coastal towns, approaching Southsea in 1986.

Right: Raising steam pressure on PS *Monarch's* new boiler for the first time, June 2013. She was returned to the water two months later.

Left: Engineer Nigel Thomas at the control station in the engine room of PS *Kingswear Castle* while the steamer is underway on the River Dart. Nigel was the only crew member to move to Dartmouth with the steamer when it was relocated there from the Medway. The only surviving coal-fired paddle steamer in British waters, *Kingswear Castle* originally had both an engineer and a stoker in the engine room. Now the engineer fulfills both roles.

Middle: Nigel lubricates the 1904 Cox & Co compound diagonal steam engine — still steaming beautifully after 110 years.

Bottom: The restored PS *Monarch* underway on the River Frome in late 2013.

LONDON & SOUTH-EAST COAST STEAMERS

ONE OF THE MOST FASCINATING social snapshots ever written about life in Victorian Britain – Henry Mayhew's *London Labour and the London Poor* from 1861 – offers many varied essays on life on the River Thames. As well as evocative and powerful accounts of the lives of the dockers and their families, Mayhew devoted a great many pages to a detailed description of the introduction and growth of steamboats on the river.

He acknowledged Fulton's steamboat on the Hudson in 1807 as being the first commerical river steamer, before describing the introduction of this new form of transport into England.

It was not until eleven years later, or in 1818, that the first English river steamer challenged the notice of the citizens as she commenced her voyage on the Thames, running daily from the Dundee Arms, Wapping, to Gravesend and back. She was called "Margery", and was the property of a company, who started her as an experiment. She was about the burden of the present Gravesend steamers, but she did not possess covered paddle-wheels, being propelled by uncovered wheels (which were at the time compared to ducks' feet) projecting from the extremity of the stern. The splashing made by the strokes of the wheels was extreme, and afforded a subject for all the ridicule

Opposite: The PS *Royal Sovereign* sets sail in the days before health and safety had even been thought of. The ship was fitted with specially-retractable funnels and masts so she could sail beneath London Bridge – her funnels seen here lowered as she departs from the quayside. She had been built at the Fairfield yard on the Clyde in 1893 for London & East Coast Express Steamship Service Ltd, and over her thirty-six years of service, was owned by several companies. This postcard, c.1906, is from her days in the colours of New Palace Steamers Ltd.

Left: A Citizen steamer tied up at Lambeth Pier in the 1860s, taken by a photographer working for James Valentine & Son on Dundee.

Above: PS *Royal Sovereign* at sea off Ramsgate, from a postcard c.1904, in her days owned by New Palace Steamers Ltd – a company originally part-owned by Fairfields.

and wit the watermen were masters of. Occasionally, too, the steamer came into contact with a barge, and broke one or more of her duck feet, which might cause a delay of an hour or so (as it was worded to me) before a jury duck-foot could be fitted, and perhaps, before another mile was done, there was another break and another stoppage. These delays, which would now be intolerable, were less regarded at that period, when the average duration of a voyage from Wapping to Gravesend by the "Margery" was about 5^1/2 hours, while at present, with favouring wind and tide, the distance from London Bridge to Gravesend, about thirty-one miles by water, is done in less than one hour and a half.

According to Mayhew, that first season was deemed a failure by the steamer's owners, but by the following summer, a new steamer, the *Old Thames*, complete with side paddle wheels, was introduced on to the river.

By 1820, four steamers were operating, and by 1830 the number had increased to thirty. In 1835, forty-three passenger steamers were registered and, by the time Mayhew was writing in 1860, that number had increased to more than one hundred.

In the 1860 edition of John Murray's definitive guide to the capital, *Murray's Handbook for Modern London: or, London as it is*, originally published a decade before Mayhew in 1851, Murray dated the first steamer on the Thames to two years earlier than Mayhew, at 1816. He also recommended to his readers that the best way to experience the glories of London was to take a steamboat trip from Chelsea to Blackwall, a journey of an hour and a half.

Initially, boatmen had to row the passengers out to the steamers, as there were yet no piers for them to embark from, but custom-built jetties soon started to appear, to the chagrin of the watermen who had seen a significant increase in their trade ferrying passengers to and from the riverbank.

Below: The 884grt PS *Koh-i-noor*, sister to *Royal Sovereign* but built at Fairfield a year earlier, is seen here heavily laden off Clacton c.1896. Despite the published date of this *Photochrom* view, she has here been photographed carrying the colours of her original owners, the Victoria Steamboat Association Ltd, under whose flag she had sailed for only the 1892-4 seasons. Like her sister, she too had retractable funnels. She passed to Palace Steamers in 1894. Laid up during the First World War, she never re-entered service and was eventually broken up at Morecambe in 1918.

Below: In this Valentine postcard of Halfpenny Pier, Harwich, c.1903, the paddle tug PS *Merrimac* is tied up at one side of the pontoon, while the GSNCo's 484grt PS *Oriole* stands on the other side. *Oriole*, completed in 1888, was the third of the five 'birds' built for GSNCo by Scott of Kinghorn. The paddle tug *Merrimac* was one of a fleet of steamers owned by R. & W. Paul, Ipswich malt merchants, and was also used as an excursion steamer during the summer, licensed to carry 172 passengers.

The first river steamers were wooden-hulled vessels, but by 1845 the first iron-hulled boats had been introduced. Amongst the first were the Westminster-based City Steamboat Company's 'Citizen' boats which were built for them at the Blackwall yard of the Ditchburn & Mare Shipbuilding Company – later to be better known as the Thames Ironworks, where so many fine vessels were constructed. Ditchburn & Mare are believed to have been the first Thames yard to build iron-hulled vessels in the late 1830s.

The remains of the yard, which employed more than 3,000 men by the late 1850s, were uncovered in 2012, a century after it closed down, during the extensive excavation work for London's new Crossrail project.

As competition on the river increased, fares reduced. The cost of the journey from Wapping to Gravesend in 1820 – three shillings (3s.0d) in the best cabin and half a crown (2s.6d) elsewhere – had halved by 1860.

Bottom: This second view of Halfpenny Pier from c.1904, shows either PS *Suffolk* or PS *Essex* taking on passengers. The steamers were built in 1895 and 1896 respectively by Earle & Co. of Hull for the Great Eastern Railway. They were both 'double-ended' to assist docking, removing the need to turn them around in the narrow confines of the River Orwell at Ipswich. *Essex* was withdrawn in 1916, *Suffolk* in 1925.

Left: R. & H. Green of Blackwall built the 996 ton PS *Duchess of York* in 1896 for the South Eastern Railway's cross-Channel service — in those days the size of steamers able to use the port of Dover was restricted by the depth of water in the harbour at low tide. Dredging the harbour in 1903 rendered her uneconomic, as the SER was able to operate much larger screw vessels on the crossing to Calais. She was scrapped in 1904.

Surprisingly, the picture Mayhew paints is of a service which, in 1860, was operating what was still very much little more than seasonal excursions – the steamers being taken out of service on the first of October, and not sailing again until Good Friday or Easter Monday.

By 1860, between 700 and 800 people were employed on the steamers or the piers and jetties which they visited. Each steamboat, Mayhew told his readers, had a crew of eight. The captain and the engineer each earned between £2 and £3 per week, the mate 30s. to 35s. A stoker earned around 30s., and the crew about 25s. each. The eighth member of the crew, known as the 'call-boy' earned a shilling per day, working six or seven days a week.

While the river steamers in Mayhew's day varied in size from between 50 tons for those on short routes, up to 180 tons for those 'adapted to run to Gravesend or beyond', by the end of the century, the average passenger steamer weighed in at over 400grt.

By the time Charles Dickens Jnr produced his *Dickens's Dictionary of the Thames* in 1887, in addition to the many steamboats working the piers and jetties along the river,

larger vessels – from the 332 passenger PS *Swift* to the 1048 capacity PS *Alexandra* – could be hired for trips to destinations as far afield as Southend, Clacton and Harwich – a steamer to carry 440 passengers from London Bridge to Clacton-on-Sea and back, mid-week, could be hired for £65.

Already there were a great many rules governing behaviour on the steamers – backed up by several Acts of Parliament – and Dickens advised his readers that

Smoking abaft of the funnel or in the chief cabin is strictly prohibited; no passengers are allowed on the bridge-boards, and passengers are particularly warned not to sit or stand on the paddle-boxes

Judging by many of the early Edwardian postcards showing heavily-laden steamers, that last instruction was later frequently ignored. Many steamers by that time had stepways and handrails over the paddle-boxes. But at the turn of the century, all was not well as far as steamer traffic on the river was concerned.

In the 1900 edition of Baedeker's *London and its Environs*, the editor suggested that

The Thames has never been adequately made use of as water-highway for passenger-service, and at present it seems not unlikely that the service will still be farther curtailed unless the City or the County Council take it in hand. The steamers ply in summer only.

Things came to a head around then, when a number of the steamer companies withdrew their services, and it was, indeed, left to the County Council to try and rectify the situation.

After a 1902 Act of Parliament, the LCC ordered a fleet of thirty paddle steamers in 1903, built at a cost of £6,000 each, and starting their commercial operation in the June 1905. In 1903, £180,000 was a substantial sum of money.

Even in those days, it would seem, local authorities recklessly believed they could make money where experienced commercial companies had failed. Not surprisingly, they too failed, and the venture was finally abandoned in December 1907. The steamers were all sold to work elsewhere – some of them, at only two years old, selling for only £500, a sixth of what they had cost to build.

Opposite top: Six of the LCC's fleet of steamers tied up near Waterloo Bridge in 1907. Whilst the identity of the three vessels closest to the camera is unknown, the three others are PS *Fitzailwin*, PS *Whittington*, and PS *Francis Drake*. The LCC had established its own service after a number of companies had failed. In 1903 they ordered a fleet of 30 steamers, half of them from Napier & Miller of Yoker on the Clyde, 10 from Thornycroft of Southampton – some of which were sub-contracted to Rennie of Greenwich – and the remainder from Thames Iron Works. Most were engined by Scott of Greenock. The service, never profitable, closed in 1907 after two years.

Left: Two of the Belle Steamers fleet, tied up at Great Yarmouth Pier, c.1903. Closest to the camera is the 1896-built PS *Southend Belle*. In the distance is the 1898-built PS *Yarmouth Belle*. Both steamers were built by Denny of Dumbarton. PS *Southend Belle* was renamed *Queen of Southend* in the 1920s, and eventually became *Thames Queen*. She was broken up in 1948. PS *Yarmouth Belle* (later renamed *Laguna Belle*) was broken up in 1946.

59

Right: PS *Christopher Wren* was built at Greenwich for the LCC by Rennie & Co in 1905, with a compound diagonal engine from Scott of Greenock. The 120grt vessel worked the route from Hammersmith Pier to Greenwich from 1907 until 1916, having been sold to the City Steamboat Co. in 1909.

Below: HRH The Prince of Wales on board the PS *King Alfred* at the opening of the LCC steamer service on 17 June 1905. As the thirty boats were identical, the same painting was used on each steamer's 'official' postcard, with just the name changed.

But if the river steamers undertaking the shorter trips were struggling, the growth of the holiday resorts around the south-east coast was hugely increasing demand for longer journeys. Throughout the closing years of the 19th century, and the whole of the Edwardian era, steamer services to Clacton, Great Yarmouth, and elsewhere around the Kent and Essex coasts experienced an annual increase in demand – resulting in the construction of some of the largest and finest paddle steamers ever built. Significant amongst the several fleets of excursion steamers which served the ports

and resorts between London and Great Yarmouth were those of the Victoria Steamboat Association (later New Palace Steamers), The General Steam Navigation Company, and Belle Steamers – although the company which operated the 'Belles' was only very briefly officially known by that name, from 1896 until 1897.

The company had started life in 1887 as the London, Woolwich & Clacton-on-Sea Steamboat Company, part-owned by the owners of Clacton Pier, operating the 241grt PS *Clacton* from 1888. Thus the company was hugely instrumental in the development of resorts such as Clacton-on-Sea itself, and their steamers did round trips from London six days a week. G.S.N.Co. vessels, on their way to Great Yarmouth, did not call in at Clacton, so the new company initially had a virtual monopoly.

As the Belle Steamers fleet expanded, their vessels also operated on the London to Great Yarmouth route. Between them, the steamers linking London with the South-east coast resorts were known locally as the 'London boats', while the Friday night and Saturday morning arrivals at Margate and Ramsgate were nick-named the 'husbands boats' so popular were they with men working in London returning home to their families for the weekend.

Below: PS *London Belle*, the largest vessel in the Belle Steamers fleet, is seen here embarking passengers at London Bridge Pier around 1908. She was built for the London, Woolwich, & Clacton-on-Sea Steamship Company by Denny Brothers of Dumbarton, and the 738grt vessel – the first in the Belle Steamers fleet to be fitted with a triple expansion engine – was launched in early March 1893. Remarkably, she entered service just three months later. Her deep draught is said to have caused her to run aground off Clacton on a number of occasions. She was eventually broken up in 1929.

Top: PS *Halcyon* at
Great Yarmouth,
c.1905. Built for the
General Steam
Navigation Company
by Scott of Kinghorn,
Fife, in 1887,
Halcyon was the first
of five boats to be
named after birds,
the others being
Mavis (1888), *Oriole*
(1888) *Laverock*
(1889) and *Philomel*
(1889) The year after
this photograph was
taken, *Halcyon* was
sold to German
owners and renamed
Cuxhaven.

Middle: Taken from
the opposite side
of the river, this
postcard from 1906
shows PS *Laverock* at
Great Yarmouth. The
fourth of the five
'birds' to be built at
Kinghorn, she
entered service in
1889 and operated
the Great Yarmouth
and Kent Coast
routes for nineteen
years before being
sold to French
owners in 1908,
subsequently sailing
out of Boulogne-sur-
Mer. She was
scrapped in 1922.

Bottom: An animated
scene at Great
Yarmouth as PS
Halcyon takes on
passengers for her
return trip to London
c.1905. To the
locals, these GSNCo.
steamers were
collectively known as
the 'London boats',
and up to five
steamers a day
arrived in the high
season.

When Belle Steamers Ltd was wound up in 1897, its assets were acquired by a new company which became known as Coast Development Ltd, and which also had interests in resorts and piers as well as the vessels themselves. With their rivals building larger and ever more luxurious vessels, the Belle Steamers fleet was expanded to keep pace, culminating in the launch of the 738grt PS *London Belle* in 1893. The majority of the 'Belles' were built for the company by William Denny & Brothers of Dumbarton, whose yard on the River Leven stood at the foot of Dumbarton Castle Rock.

Scottish-built steamers were not just the choice of Belle Steamers – the General Steam Navigation Company had a considerable number of its boats built in Scottish yards as well, but on the other side of the country, in Fife, at the Burntisland yard of Scott of Kinghorn, originally known as J. Scott & Company.

The Victoria Steamboat Association also chose a Scottish yard for their three impressive steamers – the 884grt PS *Koh-i-noor,* the 891grt PS *Royal Sovereign* and the biggest of them all at 1554grt, PS *La Marguerite* – with their choice being the Fairfield yard at Govan.

La Marguerite was built for cross-Channel work, but proved uneconomical to operate on that service, and in 1903 she was transferred to the Liverpool & North Wales Steamship Company which, like New Palace Steamers, was owned by Fairfields. She spent the next 22 years sailing from

Below; A beautiful study of the PS *Empress* reversing away from the quayside at Calais for her return trip to Dover c1903.

Right: PS *Southend
Belle* at sea, from a
postcard c.1907
published by Valentine
of Dundee.

Below right: The
double-ended 342grt
PS *Duchess of
Edinburgh* was built
by Aitken & Mansell of
Whiteinch on the Clyde
in 1884, with engines
by J. & G. Thomson
mounted side by side
between the paddles.
She worked services to
Ryde and was broken
up sometime after
1910. She is seen here
in Newhaven Harbour.

Below: The PS *London
Belle* setting off from
Tilbury to Clacton,
c.1904. Built in 1893,
she was sumptuously
fitted out, and lit
throughout by
electricity.

Left: PS *Royal Sovereign* entering Ramsgate harbour c.1905.

Below: Belle Steamers' official 1927 handbook contained details of routes and sailings.

Liverpool to the Menai Straits and North Wales resorts (for photographs of her, see the chapter *North West England and North Wales Steamers*).

Most of the cross-Channel services were operated by railway companies, with the London, Brighton & South Coast Railway introducing their first paddle steamer service sailing from Brighton to Dieppe in 1847 with the first of three steamers to carry the name PS *Dieppe*, and PS *Newhaven*.

They introduced services from Newhaven to Dieppe before 1850, and from Newhaven to Caen in the 1890s.

A major player in cross-Channel services was the London, Chatham & Dover Railway which took over the ships and services of Jenkins & Churchward in 1864.

Jenkins & Churchward had operated a Royal Mail service under contract to the Admiralty between Dover and Calais, using the paddle steamers, PS *Princess Alice*, PS *Onyx* and PS *Violet*, all built by at Blackwall by Ditchburn & Mare in 1843.

Steamer services from Dover had begun on 15 June 1821 when PS *Rob Roy* made her first passenger-carrying crossing to Calais. Local newspaper *The Kentish Chronicle* reported that there was much initial scepticism over steamers, with the majority of passengers still preferring wind rather than steam power. By August, however, the newspaper conceded that

> The Rob Roy *steam vessel continues to sail daily for France, with a number of passengers and carriages far exceeding any vessel in the employ*

Despite her very Scottish name – and having been built by William Denny – by the time the 90grt PS *Rob Roy* made her historic first crossing from Dover, she had been bought by the French railways.

With the English Channel notoriously rough at times, some highly imaginative designs were proposed to improve passenger comfort. The most adventurous was the PS *Bessemer*, built for the London, Chatham & Dover Railway at the Earle Shipbuilding & Engineering Company in Hull in 1875.

Perhaps remarkably, the era of the cross-Channel paddle steamer endured for more than a century – from the French-owned PS *Rob Roy* in 1821, until the last sailing of the 1896-built and Belgian-owned PS *Princesse Clementine* – the last paddler specifically built for cross-Channel traffic – some time before 1928. The last British-owned paddlers had all been replaced by turbine steamers before 1912.

But even as the Channel paddlers were all giving way to turbine steamers, ever-grander excursion ships were coming off the stocks at several yards – and they were still being built long after the last paddle steamer carried passengers on scheduled services to France.

The lovely PS *Golden Eagle*, built by John Brown at Clydebank – and the last new paddle steamer to be built before the start of the Great War – was launched in 1909 and served until 1951.

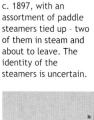
Admiralty Pier, Dover, c. 1897, with an assortment of paddle steamers tied up – two of them in steam and about to leave. The identity of the steamers is uncertain.

PS *Queen of Kent* and PS *Queen of Thanet* were both built in 1916, by Ailsa of Troon and Hamilton of Port Glasgow respectively, but as minesweepers HMS *Atherstone* and HMS *Melton*. They were converted for use as pleasure steamers in 1928 and 1929 and worked for a number of companies on the South and East coasts into the early 1950s.

The magnificent PS *Crested Eagle*, built in Cowes in 1925 did not survive her war duties and was lost in 1940, while the 1539grt PS *Royal Eagle*, the last paddle steamer to be constructed for the 'Eagle Steamers' division of the General Steam Navigation Company, and built by Cammell Laird in Birkenhead in 1932, was bigger and more luxuriously equipped than any other paddler built specifically for work on the South-east coastal routes.

Described as 'London's new Luxury Liner', her lavish interiors featured on several series of postcards all sold in the on-board sales kiosk. She was laid up in 1950, and broken up in 1953. But she was not the last paddler to take holidaymakers for their day trips from London – that honour probably goes to PS *Queen of the South* which had been built as PS *Jeanie Deans* by Fairfield of Govan in 1931, becoming one of the best-loved steamers on Scotland's Clyde coast. She first carried passengers on the Thames in May 1966, having been taken out of Clyde service at the end of the 1964 season. She

The 1213grt PS *Empress* tied up at Admiralty Pier, Dover c.1905 in the colours of the South Eastern & Chatham Railway. She was built in Govan in 1887 by Fairfield Shipbuilding & Engineering Ltd, originally for the London Chatham & Dover Railway, and worked cross-Channel services until replaced by more efficient – but no faster – turbine steamers. She was broken up in 1906.

The steam tug PS *Aid* towing two fishing smacks out of Ramsgate Harbour around 1905. Built at the Caledonian Works in Preston by William Allsup in 1889, the little tug served the port for many years. She was fitted with Napier steam capstans for heavy towing work, and Worthington steam pumps for her role as a firefighting vessel. She also supported the Lifeboat on many occasions to assist with rescue work.

Right: An unidentified steam paddle tug pulls a small brigantine out from Great Yarmouth harbour c.1900. This view was published as a tinted postcard c.1905.

Below: The wooden-hulled 107grt steam tug PS *United Service* was built by C. W. Dodgin & Company of North Shields in 1871 and purchased by the Great Yarmouth Steam Tug Company in the following year. Like many similar vessels, she spent some the winter months working as a tugboat, and in the summer operated excursions along the coast between Great Yarmouth and Cromer. She is seen here entering the harbour at Gorleston-on-Sea in the late 1920s. The vessel had a working life of 65 years before being withdrawn in 1937 and broken up in 1940.

spent her last two summers sailing to Southend before being broken up in 1967.

Other steamers arrived on the Thames, but for use as art galleries, bars and restaurants. These included both PS *Wingfield Castle*, and PS *Tattershall Castle*, built in 1934 as Humber ferries, and PS *Old Caledonia*, the former Clyde steamer PS *Caledonia*.

Wingfield Castle eventually returned to Hartlepool where she was built – see the chapter on North-east steamers – and *Tattershall Castle* is still moored by Victoria Embankment, but *Old Caledonia* was broken up after a disastrous fire in 1980. She is featured in the chapter on Scottish steamers later in this book.

Above: The GSNCo produced a series of postcards of PS *Crested Eagle* at the time she entered service in 1925, showing the steamer with a much taller funnel than other pictures of her. Her squat telescopic funnel was one of her most recognisable characteristics.

Above left: GSNCo's PS *Royal Eagle* slipping her moorings in the Thames before coming alongside Tower Pier to embark her first passengers of the day to Ramsgate, Margate or Southend. This view was published in 1932. *Royal Eagle* was one of the flottilla of vessels used to evacuate British forces from Dunkirk, making three rescue trips in 1940.

Left: The 1002grt 1896-built PS *Dover* at Dover's Admiralty Pier c.1905. She was broken up in 1911 after only fifteen years.

STEAMERS OF THE EAST & NORTH-EAST COASTS

'BEFORE WE COME HOME', wrote Louie on a postcard to his friend Willie in Chesterfeld in 1907, 'we are going on a steamer nearby like this but it is called the Frenchman.' A short excursion on the PS *Frenchman* or PS *Cambria* was, in Edwardian times, the high spot of a Bridlington or Scarborough holiday for many people.

The first paddle steamer to run excursion trips to and from the two towns was introduced in 1866. That was the 142grt PS *Scarborough* – built by Lewis & Stockwell of Blackwall in London for the Gainsborough United Steam Packet Company and powered by an oscillating 2-cylinder engine by J. Penn & Sons of London – which ran excursions from Scarborough to Whitby and Bridlington, giving passengers time ashore to explore each of the towns.

Opposite: From 1899 until she was broken up in 1927, the Hull tugboat PS *Frenchman* worked the summer season as an excursion steamer out of Bridlington, returning to her duties in Hull docks each autumn. Built in 1892 at Earle's shipyard in Hull, the 137grt, the twin-engined steamer was a highly manoeuvrable and popular vessel.

Inset: An unidentified steamer, believed to be PS *Cambria*, taking on passengers at Bridlington. A postcard dating from c.1907.

Left: In this detail from Louie's postcard to his friend Willie, two paddle steamers are disembarking passengers at the quayside in Bridlington c.1905. Nearer the camera is believed to be the paddle trawler PS *Friends* which was regularly used as a pleasure steamer in the high season.

Above: PS *Scarborough* entering Scarborough harbour around 1903.

Many of the steamers which were summer visitors to the holiday resorts worked as tugboats or trawlers out of season in the many commercial and fishing ports along the North-east coast.

Although there were many postcards which might suggest otherwise – showing crowds waiting to embark on steamers at Bridlington and Scarborough – relatively few of the paddlers on which they sailed were exclusively excursion boats.

Right: Passengers transferring from PS *Scarborough* on to small boats, Whitby, c.1903. The 1866-built Grimsby-registered steamer served the Yorkshire coast for almost half a century until broken up in 1914, her entire working life spent in the ownership of the Gainsborough United Steam Packet Company.

Left: PS *Cambria*, at Scarborough Lighthouse c.1903. Acquired by the Scarborough Harbour Commissioners in 1899, she operated excursions from 1900 until 1912.

Below: The double-ended 245grt PS *Suffolk*, on the River Orwell near Ipswich Docks c.1905, on a postcard mailed in 1907. Built by Earle of Hull in 1895 for the Great Eastern Railway, the steamer worked excursions on the Orwell. She became part of the LNER fleet in 1923 and was based at Harwich, until withdrawn in 1930 and broken up in 1931.

Regular paddle steamer services from Hull operated routes to Hamburg and other northern European ports from the earliest days of steam power, the many coastal services, for both passengers and freight operated along the north east coast from the early 1820s. The more successful routes however, were operated by screw vessels long before the supremacy of the paddle steamer started to wane.

Right: The North
Shields 'Penny Ferry',
from a postcard
c.1910.

Middle: Sail and steam
— an unidentified
paddle tug amidst
sailing ships on the Tyne
in 1907.

Below: Paddle tugs
and sailing ships
photographed against
the backdrop of the
Tyne Bridges, as a
train crosses the river.
From a postcard
published around 1903.

Left: Paddle tugs
moored on the River
Wear at Sunderland
— a detail from a
postcard c.1905.

Despite the number of tourists visiting the Victorian and Edwardian resorts of Yorkshire, Lincolnshire and the North-east, few companies built or operated fleets of larger excursion steamers to cater for them.

The Gainsborough United Steam Packet Company operated several small paddle steamers over the years – amongst them the 1854 85grt PS *Harlequin,* PS *Scarborough,* 1866, and the PS *Celia* – while the Goole & Hull Steam Packet Company's vessels were rarely more than 100grt.

North-east yards, however, had a long and distinguished history of building paddle steamers large and small for operators nationwide – amongst them the most unusual

Below: It was not
unusual for paddle
tugs to double as
ferries on occasions.
Here, one such vessel
takes on passengers
at a floating
pontoon, South
Shields c.1907.

paddle steamer ever launched, the 1974grt PS *Bessemer*, launched in 1874 at Earle's yard in Hull, for the Bessemer Saloon Steamship Company Ltd.

Designed for cross-Channel work, she was the brainchild of steel-making pioneer Sir Henry Bessemer, a sufferer from severe seasickness. In 1869 he had patented his idea for a ship which would have a unique tilting cabin, intended to keep the passenger accommodation level as the ship rolled in heavy seas.

PS *Bessemer* had four paddle wheels – two forward, two aft – powered by a pair of oscillating engines. The hydraulically-stabilised tilting cabin was controlled by an engineer manually operating the hydraulic rams while watching a spirit level.

The experiment was not a success. On her maiden Channel crossing, she hit a pier at Calais, damaging a paddle box, and on her first crossing with paying passengers, the hydraulics had to be locked off as they made the vessel even more unstable in a choppy sea. She remained moored in Dover harbour until broken up in 1879.

Earle's built several successful ferries including – for the Hull to New Holland service – the 1888 PS *Grimsby* which ran until 1922, and the two 1912-built ferries, PS *Brocklesby* and PS *Killingholme*. *Brocklesby* was withdrawn in 1936, and *Killingholme* in 1945 when the number of vessels on the route was reduced from four to three.

This cross-section of the PS Bessemer appeared on page 572 of the December 12 1874 edition of *The Graphic* magazine, and was captioned 'The New Bessemer Saloon Steamer – Transverse Section Taken Through the Saloon'. The tilting saloon had an ornate arched 20ft high ceiling and was intended to offer passengers the ultimate in luxury travel. The hydraulics were intended to counter a roll to port or starboard of up to 15°, but could do nothing to counter the rise and fall of the vessel as it rode the waves.

Top: The 556grt PS *Tattershall Castle*, built in 1934 by William Gray & Co. of Hartlepool and now moored on the Thames, has been stripped of just about everything which would identify her as a paddle steamer. How much better she would look if the outlines of her paddle boxes had been retained.

Middle: PS *Tattershall Castle* was withdrawn from service as a Humber ferry in 1973, and sold to a private buyer who converted her into an art gallery on the Thames. She arrived on the Enbankment in late 1974, and was opened by the Lord Mayor of London on 27 February 1975. Six years later she was up for sale again. Sold to Chef & Brewer, after extensive hull repairs and a complete refurbishment on the Medway, she returned to her berth and was opened as a bar and restaurant in February 1982, a role she continues to fulfill today.

Left: PS *Tattershall Castle* still has her triple expansion diagonal reciprocating engines in situ, just about visible in her dimly lit engine room. They can be viewed through small glass windows. Her owners, however, seem not to be at all interested in celebrating her history.

Right: The engines for PS *Wingfield Castle* were, like those of her sistership PS *Tattershall Castle*, built by the Central Marine Engine Works in Hartlepool, a subsidiary of William Gray & Company.

Below: The maker's plate and pressure gauges in *Wingfield Castle's* engine room identify the engine as 'CMEW' Engine No.1060. 'CMEW' stood for nothing more elaborate than the Central Marine Engine Works.

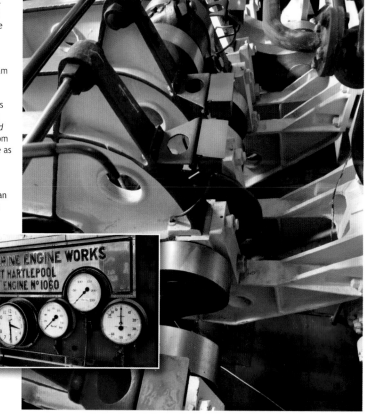

The 1914 North Shields-built tugboat PS *Eppleton Hall* under way in San Francisco Bay in 1970.

Steam paddle ferries had operated on the Humber from as early as 1814 when the 80grt PS *Caledonia,* built in Dundee by James Smart, was introduced briefly. A regular service across the river was inaugurated in 1820 with the PS *Magna Carta.*

The last paddle steamer to work the route was PS *Wingfield Castle,* one of a pair with PS *Tattershall Castle* which had been built by Gray's of Hartlepool in 1934. *Tattershall Castle* survived in service until 1969 and the 1940 Inglis-built PS *Lincoln Castle* until 1973.

After *Wingfield Castle* was withdrawn, the sole remaining Humber paddler was the 489grt DEPV *Farringford,* built in 1947 by Denny of Dumbarton – the builders and operators of the four DEPVs on the River Forth crossing until 1964. She was built for the Isle of Wight service, being transferred to the Humber in 1974, where she worked until 1981 when the Humber Bridge opened.

Wingfield Castle and *Tattershall Castle* are the only two paddle steamers from the region to survive in Britain, the former in Hartlepool, the latter as a bar and restaurant on the Thames.

Dozens of other yards from Hull to North Shields built paddle steamers and paddle tugs throughout the second half of the 19th century and well into the 20th. Amongst them were Sir W. G. Armstrong, Mitchell & Company of Elswick, Newcastle – later Armstrong Whitworth; R. Craggs & Company of Middlesbrough; C. W. Dodgin & Company of North Shields; H. S. Edwards of Howden, Wallsend; J. T. Eltringham & Company of South Shields; Hepple & Company of North Shields; M. Pearse & Company of Stockton, and J. P. Rennoldson and Sons of South Shields.

The Tyne paddle tug PS *Eppleton Hall* built in 1914 by Hepple & Co., and preserved in San Francisco, is the only surviving example of their collective output. The other survival of paddle-power in the North-east, the 1931 Paisley-built PS *John H Amos* built for work on the Tees, is in Chatham, the focus of a long-term restoration programme.

Below: PS *Wingfield Castle* at Butler's Wharf on the Thames, early 1980s. She was withdrawn from the Hull to New Holland service in 1974 and faced an uncertain future, spending three years in the ownership of the Brighton Marina Company before arriving on the Thames in 1978. She was converted into a floating bar/restaurant at Rochester, Kent, but was moved again in 1986 and is now a floating exhibit at the Hartlepool Maritime Experience *(bottom).*

Above: The distinctive funnels of P. & A. Campbell's largest steamer, the 961grt 1946-built PS *Bristol Queen*. Launched from the Bristol yard of Charles Hill & Co, she was designed as an oil-burner and fitted with a triple expansion three crank diagonal engine by Rankin & Blackmore of Greenock — virtually identical to that which still powers PS *Waverley*. She was withdrawn in 1967 and broken up in 1968

Right: The locally-built 94grt PS *Kingswear Castle* approaching Dartmouth pontoon in late March 2013 on one of her first sailings after her return to Devon.

SOUTH, WEST, &
BRISTOL CHANNEL STEAMERS

WHERE ONCE THERE WERE DOZENS of excursion steamers working the routes around the South and South-west coasts, there are now only two. Until the return of PS *Kingswear Castle* to the River Dart in 2013, there had been no paddle steamers regularly operating in this part of the country since the mid 1960s. Until 2013, only the annual visits of PS *Waverley* kept the tradition of the paddle steamer alive around the south coast and the Bristol Channel.

Kingswear Castle was completed in 1924, replacing another steamer of the same name – and using her 1904 engine. She was built on the Dart by Phillip & Son of Dartmouth, and her two-cylinder diagonal compound steam engine was built by Cox & Company of Falmouth. At only 94grt she is a small vessel, and at ninety years old at the time of writing, she is by far the oldest paddler still operating in Britain. She is also the only coal-fired paddle steamer still working in British waters – PS *Waverley* was converted to oil-burning as long ago as 1956.

Like most paddle steamers, her future seemed bleak for several years after her withdrawal from service, and there was even talk of her being broken up, but in 1967 she was bought by the Paddle Steamer Preservation Society and, after

Below left: From a lantern slide probably taken just before the Great War, the original PS *Kingswear Castle*, built by Cox & Co. of Falmouth in 1904, is seen fully laden and about to set off on a cruise along the Dart.

Below right: Two Day Excursion tickets from Cosens & Co. dating from the 1950s. If passengers ever read the small print on the tickets, they might have been nervous – with disclaimers over everything including both injury and loss of life!

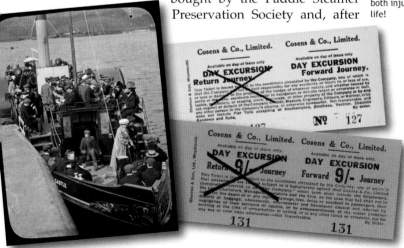

Above: Photographed at Ilfracombe Pier c.1896 and published as a postcard around 1902, from left to right are PS *Ravenswood*, built 1891, PS *Lorna Doone*, also 1891, PS *Bonnie Doone*, 1876, PS *Cambria*, 1895, PS *Westward Ho*, 1894, the 1888 Tyne-built but Cardiff-based tug PS *Earl of Dunraven*, and PS *Alexandra*, which had been built in 1854 as PS *Aquila*.

Right: On 18 July 1911, passengers about to embark on a cruise from Ilfracombe on board P. & A. Campbell's PS *Albion*, — built by J. & G. Thomson in 1892 — pose for the camera of local photographers Philipse & Lees.

four years languishing in the Isle of Wight, work started on her preservation. She was steamed again in 1982, and in 1984 she returned to passenger service once more and enjoyed a long and successful second career on the Medway, sailing out of Chatham.

A long-term deal with the Dartmouth Steam Railway and River Boat Company saw her return to her home river, and welcome her first fare-paying passengers on board on Good Friday 2013.

In the paddle steamer's heyday, the River Dart was well served by a number of companies operating services between Dartmouth and Totnes, one of the most famous, the iron-hulled *Newcomin* of 1864, being named after Dartmouth's most famous son.

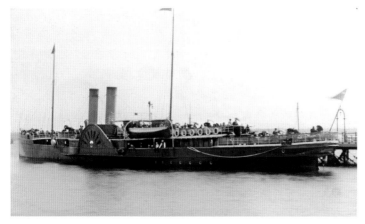

Left: The iron-hulled 283grt PS *Brodick Castle* was built by H. McIntyre of Paisley in 1878 for William Buchanan's Arran service, but was sold in 1887 to work out of Bournemouth where, for a time, she was the biggest excursion steamer working there. She is seen here in the late 1880s at an unidentified pier. Her single cylinder diagonal steam engine was already 24 years old when she was launched, having come from Buchanan's 1864 PS *Eagle*, built by Charles Connell of Scotstoun. She was broken up in 1910.

Left: The engine in the 1984-built 9grt PS *Monarch* had a long life before being adapted to drive the 42ft. paddle steamer. It was built by Lee Hurl of Tipton in Staffordshire more than a century earlier to drive an air pump at Thomas Ness's tar works in Caerphilly before being converted for use as an oil-fired marine engine by Staniforth Engineering of Rochester.

Cosens & Co.'s 1878-built 283grt PS *Brodick Castle* pulling away fully laden from Bournemouth Pier c.1906 en route for the Isle of Wight.

Both the 221grt PS *Duchess of Devonshire* — seen here reversing away from the pier at Teignmouth — and her slightly larger sister PS *Duke of Devonshire* were built at the Blackwall yard of R. & H. Green Ltd in 1891 and 1896 respectively for the Devon Steamship Company. Both were powered by compound diagonal engines by J. Penn & Sons of Greenwich. PS *Duchess of Devonshire* operated services around the South Devon coast for 43 years until lost off Sidmouth in 1934.

But paddle steamers had worked the river for three decades before *Newcomin* took to the water – the earliest recorded being the 59grt North Shields-built PS *Dart* in 1837, the year after her completion. Her owners were the Dart Steam Navigation Company. But just three years later, *Dart* was up for sale. Local attempts to purchase and operate her failed, and by 1841, she was operating out of Truro in the ownership of the Truro & Falmouth Steam Packet Company.

Despite her failure to make a return for her investors on the River Dart, however, she proved to have been the first of a long line of paddle steamers culminating in PS *Compton Castle*, built by Cox & Co. of Falmouth and in service between 1914 and 1964, PS *Totnes Castle*, 1923-64, and the 1924-built PS *Kingswear Castle* which is still in steam today.

Like *Kingswear Castle*, *Totnes Castle* was built by Philip & Son. All three were operated by the River Dart Steamboat Company.

Above: Photographed on 21 January 1957, her last day in Weymouth before being broken up in Belgium, Cosens' Southampton-built PS *Emperor of India*, ex-*Princess Royal*, had served the south coast for 50 years, 48 of them under the Cosens flag. She was withdrawn from service at the end of the 1956 season.

Left: The 483grt PS *Britannia*, seen here at Bristol c.1903, was a much changed steamer during her life. When built for P. & A. Campbell by McKnight of Ayr in 1896, she looked like this, but a rebuild replaced her saloon windows with portholes. Re-boilered in 1935, she was briefly given a squat elliptical funnel, but that was replaced in the 1940s by the twin funnels she carried for the remainder of her career.

85

The 443grt PS *Duchess of Fife* was built in 1899 by Clydebank Shipbuilding & Engineering for the London Brighton & South Coast Railway and operated between Portsmouth or Southsea and Ryde on the Isle of Wight for 30 years before being broken up in Belgium in 1929. Her profile was changed a few years after this 1903/4 view of her embarking passengers at Ryde Pier, when her upper deck housings were reconfigured. Two steamers bore this name at the time, the smaller,built by Fairfield in 1903, saw service with the CSPCo on the Clyde.

In the autumn of 2013, a second paddle steamer took to the waters of the south coast with the return to steam, after a major restoration, of the little 9grt 1984-built pleasure steamer PS *Monarch*. Since sold by Brian Waters who commissioned her, she had spent time both in the Isle of Wight and on the Tamar. She even had a starring role in the television series 'The Edwardian Farm'. The paddle steamer was, at the time, based at Morwelham Quay where the series was filmed. She did little else there, languishing on a mud bank until acquired by Noel Donnelly. She is now a visitor attraction based at Wareham Quay and operating cruises and charters down to Poole Harbour.

Splendid though both *Kingswear Castle* and *Monarch* are, and taking nothing away from the pleasure of seeing them doing what they were designed to do, neither matches in grandeur the fleets of large steamers operated by Cosens, P. & A. Campbell, the Southern Railway and many other smaller companies which once competed for passengers from the resorts and piers of the South and South-west coasts.

Cosens & Company had been established by Joseph Cosens as early as the late 1840s, with the paddle steamer *Princess*, but went on to develop an extensive network of excursions and routes before becoming a subsidiary, nearly a century later in 1946, of The Southampton, Isle of Wight and South of England Royal Mail Steam Packet Company Limited – best known as the operators of 'Red Funnel' steamers.

Between 1848 and 1946, Cosens owned and operated only twenty vessels, but their influence was considerable. Their steamers, including *Albert Victor, Emperor of India, Brodick Castle*, and others, were popular with generations of south coast holidaymakers. PS *Emperor of India*, which took part in the rescue from Dunkirk was, ironically, bought in 1908 from the Southampton-based Red Funnel line which would eventually take Cosens over in 1946.

The P. & A. Campbell fleet, operating around the South West and Bristol Channel, was established in 1889 after Peter and Alexander Campbell, the two sons of the legendary Clyde operator Captain Bob Campbell, sold their Scottish business to the Caledonian Steam Packet Company.

The two men then moved their operations to Bristol, taking with them the original 1885-built PS *Waverley* which had been constructed by McIntyre of Ayr for their father in 1885.

Between 1889 and 1967 they operated 23 paddle steamers – 11 of them new-builds – on their routes, all but one constructed in Scottish yards. Their Scottish heritage was there for all to see, with steamers named *Waverley, Glen Rosa, Albion, Bonnie Doon* and *Scotia*.

As well as their dominance of Bristol Channel services, the name of P. & A. Campbell became synonymous with excursions from Brighton when they bought the Brighton, Worthing and South Coast Steamship Company and started

Above: On a cigarette card published in 1932 PS *Britannia* – as she looked between 1921 and 1935 – can be seen tied up on the River Avon as the small cargo vessel MV *Severn Trader* is launched.

Bottom: PS *Britannia* steaming towards Ilfracombe c.1903. She held the record for the fastest crossing by a paddle steamer from Ilfracombe to Weston-super-Mare. While she spent most of her peacetime career in service between Bristol and Ilfracombe, during World War One she was on the Clyde as HMS *Briton*. World War Two saw her on the Tyne – and, as HMS *Skiddaw*, taking part in the Normandy Landings. After the war she spent two seasons on the South coast, and the early 1950s at Swansea, before being broken up at Newport in 1956.

Right: An art deco-style postcard from the Southampton, Isle of Wight and South of England Royal Mail Steam Packet Company showing three of their 'Red Funnel' steamers, the PS *Lorna Doone*, built by Napiers in Yoker in 1891, PS *Balmoral*, built by McKnight of Ayr in 1900, and PS *Stirling Castle*, built by Scott of Kinghorn in 1899. The card has, however, been printed without the vessels displaying the company's distinctive red funnels.

operating two steamers out of Brighton from the beginning of the 1902 season.

Some of the vessels which operated the Brighton service were sailed there each summer from their home port of Bristol, but others, like PS *Brighton Queen* (formerly *Lady Moyra*) and PS *Brighton Belle* (ex *Lady Evelyn*), were acquired specially for the service. The last two Campbell paddle steamers, the 1947 Fairfield-built 765grt PS *Cardiff Queen* and the 1946-built 961grt PS *Bristol Queen* were withdrawn in 1966 and 1967 respectively, and the company itself ceased

Below: Watched by crowds at Southsea's Clarence Pier, c.1906, the 443grt 1899-built PS *Duchess of Fife* sails past what appears to be the 324grt 1889-built PS *Solent Queen*.

Above: The PS *Glen Rosa* cruising off Brighton c.1904. Built for Shearer & Richie's Arran service in 1877 by Caird & Co. of Greenock, she was sold to P. & A. Campbell in 1898, and based at Brighton from 1903.

Left: The 603grt PS *Ryde* at Southampton's Royal Pier, 8 June 1969. Built in 1937 by Denny of Dumbarton, for the Southern Railway, she was withdrawn in 1969, and is now way beyond salvage at Binfield on the Isle of Wight.

Above: An animated view of Cardiff Pier Head around 1920, with two of Campbell's White Funnel steamers in view. Tied up may be the 391grt PS *Ravenswood*, built by McKnight of Ayr in 1891 — seen here with one funnel and before her saloon windows were replaced with portholes — while the 420grt 1895 Alloa-built PS *Cambria* waits offshore.

Middle: Campbell's paddle steamers embarking from below the Clifton Suspension Bridge, Bristol, c.1906.

Right: Cosens & Co.'s 173grt PS *Empress*, built in Poplar in 1879, disembarking passengers at Lulworth Cove c.1904.

operation when its last motor boats were withdrawn in 1981. PS *Bristol Queen* was the only ship in Campbell's fleet not to have been launched from a Scottish yard, having been locally built in Bristol by Charles Hill & Company.

The last of the large excursion paddle steamers was withdrawn and broken up before paddle steamer nostalgia was even in its infancy, and in any case, the logistics of maintaining and operating a vessel the size of *Bristol Queen* would have been daunting.

The abandonment and eventual destruction of a vessel like PS *Ryde*, however, is a tragedy less easy to understand.

Above: The 128grt PS *Albert Victor* taking on passengers at Weymouth c.1906. She was built in South Shields in 1883 as PS *Lass o' Gowrie*, for cruising on the Tay. She was sold to Cosens in 1889 and was broken up in 1928.

Below: The wooden-hulled 69grt PS *Mayflower* tied up at Lymington Pier, Hampshire, c.1904. Built by Marshalls of Newcastle in 1866, the smaller of two vessels on the route, she operated between Lymington and Yarmouth IOW until 1902 when she and PS *Solent* were replaced by the 130grt PS *Lymington* and the 160grt PS *Solent*. PS *Mayflower* was broken up in 1910.

91

Top: PS *Westonia*, built by Scott of Kinghorn in 1889, behind PS *Gwalia*, built by John Brown in 1905, seen in Cardiff Docks c.1908. PS *Gwalia* was renamed *Lady Moyra* when sold to the Furness Railway Co. in 1910, and changed again to *Brighton Queen* when bought by P. & A. Campbell in 1922.

Right: The 388grt PS *Princess Elizabeth*, built in 1927 by Day, Summers & Co., seen here at Torquay in May 1960. She is now used as a conference centre in Dunkerque, France.

Below right: The Cardiff and Penarth Steam Ferry Company's 1883-built 64grt double-ended PS *Iona* was built at Penarth Slipway. She operated the service with her sisters PS *Kate* & PS *La Belle Marie*.

Bottom: A paddle steamer, possibly the 129grt PS *Premier* (Denny Brothers, 1846), moored in Weymouth harbour. 1890s. The view was published as a postcard around 1905.

Above: Passengers on PS *Solent Queen*, pose for local photographers Bailey of Bournemouth as the steamer prepares to depart on a cruise to Swanage, 22 September 1921. The 324grt twin-funnelled steamer was built by Barclay Curle & Co in 1889. She continued in service until 1948.

Middle: Cox & Co of Falmouth's 1914 engine from the PS *Compton Castle* – similar to the one in PS *Kingswear Castle* – is displayed at Blackgang Chine on the Isle of Wight.

Left: The 603grt PS *Brighton Queen* was built in 1897 by Thomsons of Clydebank for the Brighton, Worthing and South Coast Steamboat Co. She was bought by Campbells in 1902, and lost in 1915 while on minesweeping duties.

Withdrawn in 1970 and used as a nightclub into the 1990s, her bridge collapsed in 2012, her superstructure is falling apart, and she is now way beyond salvation.

She would never have been cheap to restore, but she would have been worth it. If listing a vessel on the National Historic Ships Register is to serve any purpose in the future, then surely it ought to mean that destruction by neglect is not an option. And if an entry on the register is not about protection, what purpose does the list really serve?

The South coast is, however, fortunate in having two operational steamers in PS *Monarch* and PS *Kingswear Castle*. The remains of the original *Kingswear Castle* can still be seen on the mudbanks on the Dart, while the hull of her one-time sister ship, PS *Compton Castle*, languishes in Truro. *Compton Castle*'s engines – built by Cox & Co. and identical to those powering *Kingswear Castle* today – are preserved in Blackgang Chine near Ventnor on the Isle of Wight.

Top: The 1904 PS *Kingswear Castle*, built by Cox & Co. of Falmouth.

Above: Philip & Son's Dartmouth yard where the 1924 PS *Kingswear Castle* was built.

Opposite: Cox & Co.'s 1904 two-cylinder compound diagonal engine from the original *Kingswear Castle*, still powering her 1924 successor today.

Right: The heavily-laden PS *Greyhound* steaming away from Blackpool c.1904.

Passengers boarding the1894-built 1500grt PS *La Marguerite* at Llandudno for their return trip to Liverpool. Originally built for the Tilbury to Boulogne service – where her running costs proved uneconomic – she was sold in 1903 to the Fairfield-backed Liverpool & North Wales Steamship Company where she worked until 1925 cruising from Liverpool around the North Wales Coast.

NORTH WEST ENGLAND & NORTH WALES STEAMERS

DUNCAN BROWN, a young amateur photographer, was fascinated by ships and by the men who built them, and he was ideally placed to photograph those men at work, and the ships they were constructing. He lived in Glasgow but despite having been given a classical education it appears he never put his classical language skills to any use. By the mid 1850s, he had taken up amateur photography, and seems to have had ready access to Robert Napier's shipyard on the Clyde where, amongst his subjects, were groups of the leading maritime designers and steam engine builders of the day. His launch-day photograph of PS *Douglas* is one of a number of images he took in Napier's yard.

PS *Douglas* was an iron-hulled steamer, fitted with Napier's own renowned engines and boilers, and she had a reported top speed of 17 knots. She could complete the passage from Liverpool to Douglas in four hours twenty minutes.

Ordered by the Isle of Man Steam Packet Company, she was built as a direct replacement for the 1842-built wooden paddler PS *King Orry*, built in Douglas, but towed to Glasgow to be fitted with Napier engines. PS *Douglas* did not remain in the company's ownership for very long, being sold to Cunard, Wilson and Company in 1862.

The Steam Packet Company itself had been established in 1830, its first ship, the 200grt PS *Mona's Isle,* having been built by John Wood of Glasgow, her engines also coming from Napier.

Below: On the stocks at Robert Napier's Govan yard on the Clyde on 28 May 1858, with yard No.87, the 710grt PS *Douglas* is seen here on the day of her launch. Built for the Isle of Man Steam Packet Company, she became a confederate blockade ship in the American Civil War, as PS *Margaret and Jessie* before being renamed again as the USS *Gettysburg* at the end of 1863. The initial price for PS *Douglas* was £22,500, but the company paid just £17,500, an allowance of £5,000 having been given for the PS *King Orry* taken in part exchange. Photograph taken by Duncan Brown.

PS *Queen Victoria,* right, and PS *Prince of Wales,* below, were both built by Fairfield Engineering of Govan in 1887, and had originally been ordered for the Isle of Man, Liverpool and Manchester Steamship Company. In the following year, the pair of vessels were sold to the Isle of Man Steam Packet Company for a total price of £155,000. The two 1568grt vessels served the Liverpool to Douglas route until sold to the Admiralty in 1915. That deal must have seemed a real bargain. By comparison PS *Empress Queen* alone cost £130,000 new from Fairfields nine years later in 1897.

Despite commissioning several screw-propelled vessels in the 1870s, the company continued to order paddle steamers through into the 1890s, the last being the 2140grt, 2,000 passenger, PS *Empress Queen* in 1897.

Perhaps surprisingly, in 1903 they also bought the 1200grt PS *Calais/Douvres* – originally built by Fairfield in 1889 for the London Chatham and Dover Railway – from the liquidators of the failed Liverpool and Douglas Steamship Company, and operated her as PS *Mona* until 1909.

In the space of 67 years, the largest paddle steamer in the company's fleet had risen from the 200grt *Mona's Isle* to *Empress Queen* with ten times that gross registered tonnage.

Despite their being successful yards in Barrow-on-Furness, and on the Mersey – especially John Laird of Birkenhead – the majority of the paddle steamers operated

Another Fairfield-built vessel, the elegant 566grt PS *St Elvies* was built in 1896 for the Liverpool and North Wales Steamship Company Ltd, part owned by Fairfields, to carry nearly 1,000 passengers. Her two-cylinder diagonal compound engine could achieve a speed of over 18 knots sailing from Liverpool to Llandudno and around Anglesey. On occasions, she operated between Liverpool and the Isle of Man. Requisitioned for war service in 1915, she returned to her familiar North Wales routes in 1919 and was withdrawn and broken up after the end of the 1930 season. She is seen here in the Menai Straits around 1907.

by North-west companies continued to be built on the Clyde throughout the Victorian and Edwardian eras.

While the North-west had its fair share of excursion steamers from the late Victorian years right through to the outbreak of the Second World War, the majority of paddle steamers using North-western ports in the early years of steamships were commercial vessels.

The port of Liverpool operated growing trade and passenger services to the east coast of America, Canada, the Isle of Man and Ireland, with the name of Samuel Cunard foremost in the development of these routes.

Cunard's first six transatlantic paddle steamers were much smaller – and no faster – than Brunel and Guppy's 1700grt PS *Great Western* which had inaugurated Bristol to New York steamer services in 1838. What marked Cunard's service out, however, was its regularity, with scheduled fortnightly sailings ten months a year, and monthly even in the middle of winter.

Fleetwood had successful steamer routes to Belfast, the Isle of Man, and to Ardrossan on the Clyde – offering the most straightforward access to the West of Scotland in the years before the West coast railway line was completed in 1849. Those routes were served by both paddle steamers and screw-driven packet boats.

Thomas Cook had originally planned to charter the locally-owned PS *Falcon* from Fleetwood to Ardrossan to take his very first group of tourists to Scotland in 1846, but as only 350 of the expected 1200-1400 people signed up for the trip, he eventually booked them onto a scheduled overnight packet steamer instead. Such passenger services ceased just a few years after the completion of the railway link.

Above: The PS *Ivanhoe* seen passing through Barton Bridge on the Manchester Ship Canal in the summer of 1894, the year the canal opened. Remarkably, this postcard was not published until a decade later, by which time the steamer was back in Scottish waters. The Ship Canal charter had not been a success and lasted for two seasons only. The well-appointed 282grt steamer was powered by a two-cylinder diagonal oscillating engine, and was built in 1880 by D. & W. Henderson of Patrick on the Clyde. She was in service for 39 years, being withdrawn at the end of the 1919 season and broken up at Dumbarton the following year.

When the Scottish services left Fleetwood, the port concentrated on its passenger routes to Dublin and the Isle of Man, and by the gradual introduction, in the final quarter of the century, on excursion steamers linking the port with Barrow to the north, and Blackpool, Southport and Liverpool to the south.

The Furness Railway operated scheduled steamer services to Barrow using PS *Lady Margaret*, PS *Lady Evelyn*, PS *Lady Moyra* – the former South Wales steamer PS *Gwalia* – and the ex-GSNCo PS *Philomel*, but they were all withdrawn at the outbreak of the Great War, and the service was not resumed after hostilities ended.

Only the 320grt *Lady Evelyn*, built by Scott of Kinghorn in 1900, was delivered new for the service, and after the end of the war, renamed PS *Brighton Belle*, she was operated by P. & A. Campbell until lost on her second rescue trip to Dunkirk in May 1940.

For service to Ireland, the ports of Liverpool and Fleetwood had the lion's share of Belfast traffic, while Liverpool and Holyhead developed as the departure points for services to Dublin and Dun Laoghaire – then known as Kingstown – respectively. From 1824 until the end of the century the City of Dublin Steam Packet Company's paddle steamers – *Connaught, Leinster, Munster, Ulster* and the biggest of them all, *Ireland* – dominated the route, but they were withdrawn between 1896 and 1899 to make way for turbine ships.

Left: The Isle of Man Steam Packet Company's PS *Mona's Queen* leaving Fleetwood c.1905. Built by Barrow Shipbuilding Company in 1885, the 1595grt steamer operated services from Douglas to Liverpool and Fleetwood until 1929.

Middle: The identity of this paddle steamer tied up at Barrow remains uncertain. The postcard was published primarily to show the A1 submarine which had recently been refloated and repaired at Vickers Barrow works after she had sunk off Portsmouth. The card dates from c.1906.

Left: The lavishly equipped 306grt PS *Greyhound* steaming away from Blackpool's North Pier on one of her popular summer excursions, c.1904. Built by J. & G. Thomson Ltd at Clydebank in 1895 for the North Pier Steamship Company, she served the North West until sold for excursion work out of Belfast in 1923.

The Lancashire & Yorkshire Railway briefly operated a paddle steamer service from Liverpool to Ireland when it bought the Drogheda Steam Packet Company in 1902 and took over its service to Drogheda in County Louth. With the purchase came four paddle steamers, three of them from A. & J. Inglis's Pointhouse yard on the Clyde – the 1876-built PS *Tredagh*, 1878-built PS *Norah Creina* and PS *Iverna*, built 1895. The fourth, PS *Kathleen Mavourneen*, had been constructed by Wirral shipbuilders Alexander Jack & Company of Seacombe in 1885. She was one of the last ships to come out of that yard before the company declared itself bankrupt at a court hearing in Liverpool, paying its creditors just 6/8d in the pound.

The L&YR disposed of PS *Tredagh* and PS *Kathleen Mavourneen* in 1903, while *Iverna* and *Norah Creina* continued to sail until 1912. The Liverpool-Drogheda service was operated for a few more years with two 1903-built turbine steamers.

The most heavily used paddlers in the North-west throughout the Victorian and Edwardian eras were undoubtedly the Mersey ferries where the shallow draught, powerful engines, and manoeuvrability of the paddle ferry made them ideal for use at all phases of the tide. The last paddle ferry on the Liverpool-Wallasey service, the 1896-built PS *John Herron*, was withdrawn in 1919.

Pleasure steamers had a briefer golden period around the North-west coast than they enjoyed either on the South coast

Below: The 596grt 1876-built PS *Claughton* had been out of service for eight years by the time this 1902 postcard showed her at Liverpool's St George's Landing Stage. Built by D. & W. Henderson & Co. of Patrick on the Clyde, and powered by two diagonal steam engines, she served the Liverpool to Woodside route for 18 years. Her design was unusual as her funnels were sited on opposite sides of the vessel, one in front of the paddle shaft, the other behind. In 1886, she was featured on the front page of *The Illustrated London News*, crossing the river with Queen Victoria on board. Sold in 1894, she was renamed *Australia* and worked as a tug on the newly-opened Manchester Ship Canal until broken up in 1899.

Paddle-power drove many of the Mersey ferries well into the 20th century.

Top: The Mersey ferry PS *Mayflower* passing PS *Thistle* in mid-river in 1904. *Mayflower* had originally been built as a 'luggage boat', but was converted for passenger traffic in the 1880s. By the time PS *Thistle* was launched, by Scott of Kinghorn in 1891 the ferry company had been using srew-driven ferries for some years, so she was something of a throwback in terms of design.

or on the Clyde, and paddle steamers did not endure for anything like the total steamer era. Many of the more popular excursion services were taken over by screw turbine steamers long before the Second World War. Indeed, not a single excursion paddle steamer was in operation around the North-west or North Wales after 1940, the last year the PS *King George* ran excursions from Conway. Only a little over a dozen were still operating in the region into the 1920s. The

Middle: Paddle steamer ferries and tugs at Liverpool's Pier Head c.1905.

Bottom: Wallasey Ferries' 361grt PS *Violet*, built by William Allsup at the Caledonian Works in Preston, was the last iron-hulled paddle steamer built for the Wallasey to Liverpool crossing, sailing from 1884 to 1901. Her design was based on that of the PS *Heatherbell*, the company's first twin-funnelled steamer which had entered service twenty years earlier. The structure atop the paddle box was the captain's observation station when supervising the two-level embarkation and disembarkation of passengers.

Right: Two of the
Furness Railway
Company's steamers,
PS *Lady Margaret* and
PS *Lady Evelyn* at
Ramsden Quay, Barrow
c.1905. The 369grt
PS *Lady Margaret* was
built in 1895 by
McMillan of Dumbarton
and purchased second-
hand from P. & A.
Campbell in 1903.
The 320grt PS *Lady
Evelyn* was ordered
new by the company
from Scott of Kinghorn
in 1900.

Below: PS *Bickerstaffe*
was built in 1879
by John Laird at
Birkenhead for
Blackpool operater
John Bickerstaffe,
Yard No.455, for
service initially with
his Blackpool, Lytham
and Southport Steam
Packet Company Ltd.
She ran excursions out
of Blackpool, with
occasional longer trips
to the Isle of Man, for
49 years before being
withdrawn and broken
up in 1928. From 1895
she was operated
by John's son Thomas
Bickerstaffe's
Blackpool Passenger
Steam Boat Company
Ltd, based in
Fleetwood. The
Bickerstaffe family
would, in 1894, ensure
their lasting place in
seaside history when
they built the famous
Blackpool Tower.

little steamers PS *Belle* and PS *St Trillo* were withdrawn in 1921, the 198grt *St Trillo* – built in 1876 as PS *Carisbrooke* – being converted into a steam yacht and ending her days as PS *San Telmo*.

The 147grt PS *Belle*, built in Plymouth in 1892 by Willoughby Brothers for the Llandudno & Carnarvon Steamboat Co Ltd as PS *Belle of Llandudno*, had spent almost all of her career running excursions out of Blackpool and Southport. PS *Greyhound* and PS *La Marguerite* were both withdrawn in 1925 from North Wales and Blackpool sevices respectively, followed in 1928 by the Blackpool stalwart PS *Bickerstaffe*.

The double-ended 171grt Liverpool-built PS *Pearl*, the last of a trio of paddle steamers introduced to operate the 6 mile sailing from Liverpool to the pleasure gardens at Eastham Ferry, was withdrawn in 1929 after 32 years in service. She was the last paddle steamer to operate regularly on the Mersey.

The 338grt PS *Snowdon*, built by Laird of Birkenhead for the Snowdon Steamship Company's service from Liverpool to North Wales was broken up in 1931, having been withdrawn the previous year – the same year 566grt PS *St Elvies* was last operated by the Liverpool & North Wales Steamship Company.

While other services were closing, the PS *Jubilee Queen* was introduced to the North-west at the beginning of the 1935 season. She had been built in 1897 by Day Summers & Co of Southampton as PS *Duchess of Kent*, before becoming PS *Clacton Queen* in 1934, and *Jubilee Queen* in the following year. She operated between Liverpool and Blackpool for just one season, being withdrawn at the end of 1936, the same year the 1891-built 24grt Conway steamer PS *Prince George* was withdrawn from service.

The Ormes Cruising Company Ltd bought the 1888-built PS *Lady Orme* – the Paisley-built former MacBrayne steamer PS *Fusilier* – when she was 49 years old, and operated her for the 1937 and 1938 seasons. She spent her last few months under new owners – and a third name – as PS *Crestawave*, and when she too was withdrawn, the era of the excursion paddle steamer around the North-west and North Wales coasts was at an end.

However powerful and highly versatile paddle tugs outlived them all, continuing to work North-west ports and the Manchester Ship Canal until replaced by diesel vessels in the early 1950s. Just one example of them all survived – 'saved' by the National Maritime Museum – until she too was broken up in 1999, the engines now being all that remain of the 1907-built PS *Old Trafford*.

Below left: The starboard engine from the 1907 paddle tug *Old Trafford*, later renamed *Reliant*, survives in the National Maritime Museum in London. She was built in 1907 by J. T. Eltringham & Company of South Shields for the Manchester Ship Canal Company, with engines by Hepple & Company also of South Shields. She was used between Eastham and Manchester until 1951, one of more than twenty paddle tugs to work the canal. In 1951 she was sold and re-named, ending her days in 1969 in Seaham Harbour. She was displayed at the museum until 1996 and dismantled in 1999.

Below: The port engine of PS *Old Trafford/Reliant* is preserved at Markham Grange Steam Museum.

SCOTTISH COASTAL, RIVER AND LOCH STEAMERS

SCOTLAND WAS THE BIRTHPLACE of the commercial paddle steamer, and also home to the shipyards which built many of the excursion steamers which dominated coastal transport around Britain's coasts throughout the Victorian and Edwardian eras. A Scottish yard – A. & J. Inglis at Pointhouse on the Clyde – also constructed the last large paddler ever built in Britain. At the time of writing, that steamer, the PS *Maid of the Loch* completed in 1953, is undergoing restoration at Balloch on the shores of Loch Lomond.

Pointhouse is now the site of Zaha Hadid's spectacular new Glasgow Museum of Transport, although it is a sailing vessel – the *Glenlee* – rather than a paddle steamer which is tied up at the quayside. *Waverley* is the only other surviving paddle steamer in Scotland, from the many hundreds which were launched down the slipways of Clyde yards. Indeed, only five steamers in total are currently in Scottish waters – the 1901-built SS *Sir Walter Scott* on Loch Katrine, the 1943 puffer *VIC32* and HMY *Britannia* from 1953 all being screw-driven rather than paddlers. Plans to launch a new steamer *Spirit of the Tay* on to Loch Tay a few years ago ended in failure.

Opposite and below: Often celebrated as 'the last sea-going paddle steamer in the world', the PS *Waverley* was built on the Clyde in 1947 by A. & J. Inglis for the LNER. The 693grt vessel is powered by a three-crank, diagonal, triple-expansion, engine.

Inset: An excursion paddle steamer takes tourists out to see work progressing on the final stages of the construction of the Forth Bridge, 1889.

The 120grt PS *Mary Jane* taking on passengers and cargo at Tarbert on Loch Fyne, photographed by Duncan Brown in 1856. Built in Glasgow by Todd & McGregor in 1846, she had a working life of 85 years, most of them sailing as PS *Glencoe* for the Loch Fyne Steam Packet Company after she was extensively rebuilt in 1875, her gross tonnage being increased to 175. At the time she was withdrawn, she and PS *Premier* were the oldest working paddle steamers in the world.

The paddle steamer quickly became the most accessible means of travel in Victorian Scotland – where there were very few railway bridges across rivers, and in many places, as yet no reliable roads.

Thomas Bouch – he of Tay Bridge Disaster infamy – pioneered what he called the 'floating railway' – the world's first roll-on roll-off paddle steamer twin-track train ferries – from Granton to Burntisland, as early as 1850. The first vessels were Robert Napier's 399grt 1849-built PS *Leviathan*, the 1850 PS *Robert Napier*, and the 1851 PS *Balbirnie*. The service continued until the opening of the Forth Bridge, largely carrying coal from Fife to Edinburgh. Further north, the Tay got a Ro-Ro train ferry – the 243grt PS (or TF) *Carrier* – in 1858.

Coastal steamer traffic became the normal means of transporting farm produce, mail and the everyday requirements of life as well as passengers. Quickly, a relatively small number of players dominated the market, building ever larger, faster and more luxurious steamers to service their routes. By the end of the 19th century, there were hundreds of vessels working the networks of routes which serviced Scotland's west coast and her islands. And the steamer networks were quickly dominated by a few large operators.

There can be few businessmen about whom little ditties have been written – and even fewer who have been the subject of rewritten psalms! One of those, David MacBrayne, ticks both boxes!

On Scotland's late Victorian West coast, the usually God-fearing locals even modified the 24th Psalm to give a sense of his omnipotence!

The Earth belongs unto the Lord, and all that it contains.
Except the Kyles and the Western Isles, for they are all
MacBrayne's.

By the 1890s, there were several other variants on the same theme, one of which – in slightly less lyrical terms – seemed even to exclude God's influence over the man's monopoly

Top: The twin-engined PS *Carradale*, seen here in 1856, was well known around the ports of Kintyre. She foundered off Luing Island on 18 June 1866 and was lost.

Above: Paddle tugs towing sections of the second Tay Bridge, photographed by one of the photographers from Valentine of Dundee, 1885.

Right: A paddle tug guides a sailing vessel into Leith docks around 1900.

Below: The 160grt paddle tug *Empress of India* was built in 1877 for William Strong of Cardiff and sold for use in Leith Docks in 1893. This 'bromoil transfer' print was created by eminent photographer Alexander Wilson Hill around 1910.

O'er Heav'n and Earth The Lord God reigns
But the Western Isles,
They're David MacBrayne's.

The message was clear – this was one very important man whose power, should he ever be tempted to abuse it, was great enough to bring the West coast of Victorian Scotland grinding to a halt.

David MacBrayne, of course, owned a large number of the passenger steamers plying the coast, and his paddle steamers – and the people and goods they carried – were the lifeblood of the islands and the remote communities peppered along the shores of Scotland's western sea lochs.

The company which still carries MacBrayne's name can trace its origins back 160 years and is still at the heart of travel off Scotland's West coast today. When it was established in 1851, it was as David Hutcheson & Company, and MacBrayne was a junior partner. His pedigree, however, was high – he was the nephew of the brothers George and James Burns, whose shipping empire was already substantial. Hutcheson was a cousin of the Burns brothers, and it was the decision of George and James to divest themselves of their local shipping interests and concentrate on transatlantic traffic which gave Hutcheson and MacBrayne the opportunities they needed.

David Hutcheson & Company acquired the Scottish interests of G. & J. Burns and, as they say, never looked back. The Burns retained their lucrative Irish Sea services from Ardrossan to Belfast. In 1877, Hutcheson retired, and his brother Alexander left the company in 1879 leaving MacBrayne as sole owner.

By the late 1880s, more than fifty paddle steamers worked the River Clyde alone, visiting, between them, over eighty piers and jetties, and carrying several million passengers. Even at the outbreak of the Great War, there were more than forty steamers in service on the river.

PS *Undine* at the Broomielaw, photographed by G. W. Wilson of Aberdeen, in the late1870s.

Right: Sailing past the Wallace Monument near Stirling c.1903, the appropriately-named PS *Stirling Castle* served the river for only eight years before being sold to the Southampton, Isle of Wight & South of England Royal Mail Steam Packet Company, subsequently sailing out of Bournemouth. Built in 1899 by Scott of Kinghorn, the 271grt steamer's original owners were the Galloway Steam Packet Company.

Below: Steamers tied up at Lochgoilhead Pier, from a postcard published c.1904. The vessel nearest the jetty is the Lochgoil & Inveraray Steamboat Company's 234grt PS *Edinburgh Castle*, built in 1879 by Robert Duncan of Port Glasgow, with engines by Rankin & Blackmore. The vessel was scrapped in 1913.

Prices – never cheap – had, of course increased substantially over the intervening quarter century. In 1888, a return ticket from the Broomielaw to Dunoon had cost two shillings (10p) in the cabin, and one and sixpence (7.5p) 'steerage' which in Clyde steamer parlance meant on deck. By 1914, most steamers had two saloons – effectively first class and second class accommodation – and an afternoon cruise from Broomielaw to Dunoon cost half a crown (12.5p) in the more luxurious aft saloon, and two shillings (10p) in the fore saloon. That may not seem a lot, but when you consider that the average wage in Edwardian times for a semi-skilled worker was probably rarely more than thirty shillings (£1.50) a week, and even the head teacher of a medium-sized school could expect no more than £4 a week, those fares were high enough to make a trip 'doon the watter' a special treat. At today's prices, that afternoon steamer trip to Dunoon would cost about £25 even in the cheap saloon!

By comparison, an excursion in 2013 from Dunoon to Rothesay on the 1947-built PS *Waverley* – the last sea-going paddler in the world, cost just £19.

And yet, despite those prices, steamers departed every few minutes from Broomielaw from just after six in the morning until well into the evening, some on short trips, but others doing the long hauls to Inveraray, Campbeltown, Lochgoilhead and other outposts of the network, some doing the runs non-stop, but others stopping at numerous piers along the way.

Passengers joining the PS *Lord of the Isles* at Dunoon or Wemyss Bay could enjoy five star catering in the luxurious dining saloon if they could afford it. A breakfast fit for a king could be purchased for two shillings, a four-course luncheon for three shillings, and a 'high tea' for two shillings. Those enjoying such rich fare would probably be the same people who travelled from Glasgow in a first class railway carriage to meet the steamer, and paid seven shillings and sixpence (37.5p) for the privilege!

There were exceptions – low-cost excursions from Glasgow in the 1880s offered the chance to sail to Garelochhead and back – with an hour on shore – for the sum of ninepence on deck, or one shilling in the cabin. The steamer left at 3pm and returned at 10pm! For the same price, Glaswegians could enjoy a three hour sail to Dunoon and Largs, stopping at Partick, Renfrew, Bowling,

Ten steamers laid up for the winter at Greenock's West Quay, from a postcard published around 1904. Included in the group of Caledonian Steam Packet Company steamers are PS *Ivanhoe*, built by D. & W. Henderson in 1880, PS *Duchess of Hamilton*, Denny Brothers 1890, and PS *Galatea*, built in 1889 by Caird of Greenock.

Dumbarton, Greenock and Gourock. The fare was the same irrespective of which pier the passengers chose to disembark, but of course the shorter the sail, the more time ashore. Going all the way to Largs gave them only half an hour ashore before starting the three-hour sail back to Broomielaw.

Excursions to special events were an occasional opportunity to combine a sail with the chance to see something really spectacular. One such event was the huge fireworks display organised at Wemyss Bay on the night of Friday 22 August 1890, for which the Caledonian Steam Packet Company organised a fleet of steamers to bring holidaymakers from numerous resorts along the banks of the river, and from the resorts on Bute and Arran.

The fireworks display was organised by Brocks – one of the country's leading manufacturers of the day (and which survived until taken over by Standard Fireworks almost a century later) – and included one of the spectacular displays which they had previously organised at the Crystal Palace in Sydenham and which no doubt many of those attending the Wemyss Bay spectacle had read about.

Described as 'The Great Crystal Palace Sensation', the display entitled 'MAN THE LIFEBOAT' was perhaps not the best one for an audience a large proportion of which was watching from on board steamers many of which notoriously had very few lifeboats themselves!

Opposite page: The paddle ferry *Forfarshire* was built for the Firth of Tay crossing between Dundee and Newport by Gourlay of Dundee in 1863, and served the river for thirty years. In 1893 she was sold to operators on the Forth, and spent 27 years on that service. Her very tall funnel, was added during her 1904 refit.

Inset: PS *Dundee*, built by Simons of Renfrew in 1875, arriving at Dundee Slipway, 1904.

Below: PS *Dundee* at the Newport-on-Tay slipway, also c.1904.

Top: The Burntisland to Granton ferry PS *William Muir*, berthed at Burntisland c.1905. By the time the card appeared, the 364grt steamer, built in 1879 by John Key & Sons of Kinghorn, had been reconfigured with a single funnel. She was just three months old when she took on the task of returning the bodies of those lost in the Tay Bridge Disaster.

Middle: MacBrayne's PS *Gairlochy*, seen here on the Caledonian Canal, had started life in 1861 as PS *Sultan*, spent three years as PS *Ardmore*, becoming *Gairlochy* when bought by MacBrayne in 1894.

Bottom: PS *Lucy Ashton*, built 1888, at Arrochar, Pier, Loch Long, c.1904. In the 1950s, her hull was used to test an experimental jet engine.

Advertised as 'The Most Magnificent DISPLAY OF FIREWORKS EVER EXHIBITED IN SCOTLAND' spectators could get to Wemyss Bay by special trains direct from Glasgow for three shillings first class or two shillings second class, or by train as far as Gourock then transferring to either the PS *Duchess of Hamilton* or PS *Ivanhoe* – from which they would view the display – for the same price. Other steamers brought visitors from Helensburgh, Kirn, Dunoon, Inellan, Kilcreggan, Largs, Rothesay, Millport, Lamlash, Whiting Bay and numerous other piers. Passengers from all the piers on Bute arrived off Wemyss Bay on board the company's newest steamer *Galatea*, which was heralded as a new era in Clyde transport, but which fell out of favour and was sold in 1906.

While the success of the steamer network as a means of getting from one place to another was probably never in

Two views of David Macbrayne's 1878-built, 601grt PS *Columba*. The largest Clyde steamer ever built, she was said to be the most luxurious and well equipped paddle steamer on the river. Built by J. & G. Thomson at Clydebank, she was steel-hulled, and operated mainly on the Glasgow to Ardrishaig 'Royal Route'. In the first view, *left*, from a glass lantern slide c.1890, she is seen approaching Tarbert, while the lower view shows her embarking passengers at Tarbert Pier around 1904. Sold at the end of the 1935 season after sailing for 55 years, she was broken up at Dalmuir on the Clyde.

Right: MacBrayne's PS *Mountaineer* built in 1852 by J. & G. Thomson at Govan, and seen here getting up steam at Corpach Pier, had been lost off Oban in 1889 more than a dozen years before this postcard was published.

Below: PS *Fusilier* took on the Oban to Fort William service in 1889. Photographers loved this viewpoint

doubt, the growing popularity of just going for a sail proved a highly profitable additional source of income for the Victorian investors.

By the dawn of the 20th century, cruise passengers had undoubtedly become just as important a part of their business plan as taking people from A to B. Indeed, in the early years of the 20th century, many of the routes barely broke even – so in those cases the cruise passengers were vital.

Competition amongst the companies was reminiscent of the years following bus deregulation in the 1980s – steamer captains going to considerable lengths to arrive first at a pier

The Glasgow and Inveraray Steamboat Company's 1877-built PS *Lord of the Isles*, seen here at Inveraray Pier in the 1880s.

in order to get as many passengers on board often took risks involving their own boats, the boats they were trying to overtake, and the piers they were approaching at unsafe speeds. Just like our own experience of buses, there would be none for ages, then two or three would come along at once! Some captains were repeatedly in trouble for this practice, suffering heavy fines. But, despite this and the often considerable overloading of their vessels, the Clyde steamers remained a very safe and reliable mode of transport indeed.

Other methods of attracting customers were perhaps more surprising. Notable amongst these was the growing number of 'dry boats' in the closing years of the 19th century. The temperance movement was enjoying a considerable popularity at the time, and many Clyde resorts had temperance hotels on their promenades or main streets. But the popularity of the dry boats was by no means restricted to those who had a fundamental aversion to drink. Far from it – their popularity with parents who did not wish themselves or their children to be subjected to the public excesses of those who started drinking on board as soon as the bar opened made them the family boats of choice.

By the end of the Victorian era the Clyde coast was dominated by railway company steamers, but MacBrayne's and the Caledonian Steam Packet Co – which had been set up in 1889 by the Caledonian Railway – effectively controlled the routes to the islands.

Top: The 319grt PS *Kylemore*, in the colours of Captain John Williamson, setting off from Glasgow's Broomielaw c.1910 with few people on board, pulls out past MacBrayne's PS *Columba*, built in 1878. PS *Kylemore* had been built by Russells of Port Glasgow and sold to the Hastings, St Leonards & Eastbourne Steamboat Company, initially sailing as PS *Britannia*. Sold to the Glasgow & South Western Railway in 1904, she became PS *Vulcan*. Her final name change came in 1908.

Right: From a few years earlier, here we see PS *Vulcan* in the colours of the G&SWR passing what is thought to be PS *Viceroy* moored at the Broomlielaw. In 1906, *Viceroy* was sold becoming *Rhos Colwyn*.

Rivalry was intense, and the quest for success led to the construction of some of the finest paddle steamers of the age. The companies vied with each other to offer more frequent services, faster sailings, greater comfort, and ever-better on-board facilities.

MacBrayne's – and Hutcheson's before them – were responsible for building some of the fastest and finest steamers, many of them bearing names which have continued to be used throughout the fleet. In 1855 they commissioned the first steamer to carry the name *Iona* – built especially for what had become known as the Royal Route to the Isles. *Iona* was sold after seven years and was used to run the blockade during the American Civil War. Her replacement of the same name was also sold to the Americans, but sank off Lundy on her outward journey. *Iona* number three was launched in 1864 and served the company for over forty years. She was the last paddler to carry the name.

The most recent *Iona* – the seventh, introduced in 1970 – was the first of a new generation of drive-through Ro-Ro ferries designed for the age of the motorcar.

MacBrayne also operated another 'Royal Route' – from Glasgow to Inverness via Ardrishaig, Oban and Fort William – so named because Queen Victoria had made just such a journey in 1847. On that service, according to the company's 1897 timetable, it was possible to leave Glasgow on board the PS *Cavalier* at 1pm on a Monday, and disembark at Muirtown Locks at Inverness by 4pm on Wednesday. The 1897

Opposite page bottom: The PS *Galatea*, in steam from a postcard published around 1903. The 331grt vessel, built for the Caledonian Steam Packet Company by Caird & Company of Greenock in 1889 – the first Clyde steamer to be fitted with large compound steam engines – was hugely powerful, but expensive to operate. She was sold to an Italian owner in 1906, and broken up in 1913.

Below: PS *Vulcan* again, this time pulling out past David MacBrayne's PS *Iona*. Built in 1864 by J & G Thomson at Clydebank, the 396grt *Iona* was MacBrayne's third vessel to carry that name. She was built for the Glasgow to Ardrishaig and Glasgow to Oban 'Royal Routes', services she shared with PS *Columba* after 1878. She also undertook excursions from Greenock during her 71 year career. This postcard, c.1905, is charmingly captioned 'Off Down the Water, Glasgow' instead of the local description 'off doon the watter'.

timetable promised that "cabs and omnibuses from the different hotels await the steamer's arrival at Muirtown." For those with the time and the money to afford such a trip, the company advertised that the overnight cabins on the vessel were equipped with electric lights! The round trip fare "with first-class sleeping accommodation" cost 40/-, or 70/- with all meals included! Along the way *Cavalier* – one of MacBrayne's 'Swift' steamers under the command of Captain D. McTavish – put in at no fewer than nineteen piers!

By the early years of the 20th century, and the arrival of the age of the postcard, steamer companies quickly realised that selling postcards of their vessels was a good way of earning publicity and promoting their routes. Our fascination with ships continues to this day, and postcards of CalMac's latest ships are still sold on board.

David MacBrayne retired in 1905 and his two sons took over the business, but in the years after the First World War the company started to experience considerable financial problems. This led to ownership passing to Coast Lines Ltd and the London, Midland & Scottish Railway, merging with the Caledonian Steam Packet Company, and eventual nationalisation sailing under the Caledonian MacBrayne name. And so it was that the MacBrayne name was carried

Opposite page: This detail from a postcard produced to mark the opening of the Caledonian Railway's new Wemyss Bay railway station in 1903 shows the Rothesay boat about to depart. The steamer is either the 244grt PS *Caledonia*, built in 1889 in the Port Glasgow yard of John Reid & Company, or her sister, the 246grt PS *Marchioness of Breadalbane*, launched from the same yard in the following year. Both were powered by Rankin & Blackmore engines. The two vessels were subsequently requisitioned for service in the First World War, returning to the Clyde after hostilities ended. PS *Caledonia* served until 1933, PS *Marchioness of Breadalbane* until 1935 when she was sold as an excursion steamer working out of Great Yarmouth. She was broken up in 1937.

on the company's last paddle steamer, the *Waverley*, until it was sold in 1973 to a trust for one pound.

For many package tour visitors to Scotland – from Victorian times right up to the 1970s – their main contact with steamers would be on the country's inland lochs – paddle steamers on Loch Lomond, and screw steamer – *Rob Roy* and later *Sir Walter Scott* – on Loch Katrine. There they would embark for a sail along some of the country's most spectacular stretches of water, while being entertained to what the package holiday organisers believed to be a truly Scottish experience – inevitably involving bagpipes.

As far as can be ascertained, however, while there were steamers on Lochs Awe, Katrine, Lomond and Tay from as early as the 1860s, only Loch Lomond was host to paddlers. On the other lochs, the steamers were all screw-driven.

Loch Lomond's first paddle steamer, David Napier's PS *Marion* had been introduced on to the loch experimentally as early as 1818, just six years after Bell's *Comet* had first sailed on the Clyde. Indeed, *Marion*, built by William Denny and Archibald MacLachlan at Dumbarton, had herself first sailed on the Clyde, plying between Greenock and Glasgow in 1817, and like *Comet*, she sported a tall funnel which also served as a mast. She was introduced on to the loch the

Left: PS *Glen Sannox* at sea c.1910. A large vessel, the 610grt *Glen Sannox* was built by J. & G. Thomson at Clydebank in 1892 for the Glasgow & South Western Railway, and worked the Arran service for a series of owners until scrapped in 1925. She had a high top speed, but proved expensive to operate.

Right: In this tinted lantern slide from the early 1880s, the 235grt PS *Benmore* is just pulling away from the Broomielaw for her regular service to Kilmun. Built in 1876 by T. B. Seath of Rutherglen for Captain Bob Campbell, she operated this service until sold to William Buchanan in 1885, after which she was more usually operated on the service to Rothesay. She operated on charter to the Caledonian Steam Packet Company from 1915 until 1920, and was broken up in 1923.

Below right: The 306grt PS *Minerva* taking on passengers at Greenock's Princes Pier, c.1903. Built in 1893 by J. & G. Thomson of Clydebank, she served Rothesay and the Kyles of Bute for the Glasgow & South Western Railway from Greenock or Ardrossan until 1914. Requisitioned for war service, she was captured by Turkish forces in 1917, and broken up in Turkey about ten years later.

Left: Coaches and charabancs from local hotels awaiting the arrival of one of MacBrayne's steamers at Muirtown Locks on the Caledonian Canal near Inverness c.1904.

following year, remained in service until 1827, and was wrecked in 1832. Her engine casings had been built at David Napier's Camlachie Foundry in Glasgow. She would be followed, over the following century and a half, by a long list of ever-larger paddlers to cater for the growing Trossachs tourist trade.

The Morning Chronicle, in its edition for May 5, announced her return to the loch in 1819 – "THE MARIAN STEAMBOAT will begin to PLY through LOCH LOMOND on the 1st day of June, and continue to do so every lawful day during the Summer calling at Balmaha, Luss, Rue-Ardennan, foot of Benlomond, Tarbet, and Rob Roy's Cave, leaving Balloch every morning at ten o'clock and returning in the evening."

An account of a journey on board the 60ft steamer was carried in *Airy Nothings; or, Scraps and Naughts and Odd-cum-shorts; in a Circumbendibus, Hop, Step and Jump by Olio Rigmaroll*, published in 1825, but in promotional flyers for the

A contemporary print of PS *Marion* on Loch Lomond, a piper playing before the mast/funnel.

This view of PS *Neptune* entering Ayr harbour in the late 1890s was not published as a postcard until c.1904. She initially operated services from Greenock's Princes Pier to Rothesay, the Kyles of Bute and Ardrossan, but had been replaced at Greenock by the larger and faster PS *Jupiter* in 1896, after which she was used by the G&SWR as a cruise ship. Like her sister ship PS *Mercury* (see opposite) she was built in 1892 at Yoker by Napier, Shanks & Bell. Both vessels were driven by compound diagonal steam engines built in Glasgow at the Elliot Street Engineering Works of David Rowan & Son Ltd.

service, her name appears as 'Marion'. It is interesting to notice in Michael Egerton's engraving of the steamer (*p125*), that even as early as 1825, such journeys were accompanied by the ubiquitous piper – he can be seen standing just in front of the mast, resplendent in his red jacket.

Writing in his 1863 book *A Tour in Tartan-land*, the humourist and *Punch* contributor Cuthbert Bede – the pseudonym of the Reverend William Bradley – described just such a sail on Loch Lomond, remarking that "The blind fiddler, who was also on board, and to whose merits a printed testimony had been posted up by the cabin door, was a mitigated nuisance; but the bagpiper was an unmitigated evil, and ought never have been permitted to walk the deck."

The Reverend Bradley did not name the boat on which he sailed, but there were three steamers in service in the autumn of 1862 when he visited the loch – the 93grt PS *Queen Victoria*, built at Denny's yard in 1852, the 1858-built 142grt PS *Prince of Wales*, or the brand new and much larger 169 grt PS *Prince Consort*. *Prince of Wales* had been built at the Port Glasgow yard of Lawrence Hill & Co., while *Prince Consort* had been constructed at the Greenock yard of Caird & Co. The *Queen Victoria* was in service only from 1852 until 1868, *Prince of Wales* from 1858 until 1901, and *Prince Consort* from 1862 – introduced just a few weeks before Bradley's visit – until 1881.

Opposite bottom: 537grt PS *Neptune* cruising off Dunoon c.1905. Built in 1892 for the Glasgow & South Western Railway Company, she operated services to Arran and Bute from Greenock. As a minesweeper off Dover in the First World War – and renamed HMS *Nepaulin* – she was mined and sunk in 1917.

Naming a steamer was an important part of attracting passengers, and the huge popularity of Sir Walter Scott's writings made his book titles and characters obvious choices for the steamer companies. *Rob Roy*, and *Sir Walter Scott* on Loch Katrine may have been screw steamers, but there were plenty other names to be exploited by the operators of west coast paddle steamers. The majority of them were built by A. & J. Inglis at Pointhouse, and operated by the North British Steam Packet Company – later the North British Railway.

Amongst the Inglis-built steamers whose names were drawn from Scott's novels were *Meg Merriles* (1866-1908), two steamers carrying the name *Talisman* (1896-1934 and 1935-1966), *Marmion* (1906-1941), *Fair Maid* (1915-1916) and *Kenilworth* (1898-1937).

And, of course, there was also *Waverley*, the last of which is still sailing today. In fact four paddlers have carried that name, one of which, although built by John Brown, spent her entire life operating under the flag of P. & A. Campbell on the South coast of England.

The North British Railway also operated PS *Redgauntlet* (1895-1934), built by Barclay Curle & Co.; PS *Lady Rowena* (1891-1922) built by McKnight of Ayr; PS *Lucy Ashton* (1888-1949) built by Seath & Co. of Rutherglen; and PS *Diana Vernon* (1895-1926), also built by Barclay Curle, which was sold in 1899 and subsequently renamed *Worthing Belle*.

Above: This beautiful hand-tinted lantern slide was produced in 1892, the year PS *Mercury* entered service for the Glasgow & South Western Railway on their Greenock to Rothesay service. The 248grt steamer was built at Yoker by Napier, Shanks & Bell, and had a top speed of 18 knots. She served as a minesweeper in the Great War, and returned to the Clyde from 1920 to 1934. She was broken up in Barrow in 1937.

Opposite page: PS *Maid of the Loch* undergoing restoration at Balloch Pier in the late 1990s.

Inset: PS *Maid of the Loch* at Inversnaid Pier, June 15 1968, in Caledonian Steam Packet Company colours of white hull and buff funnel.

This page top: PS *The Queen*, right, at Balloch c.1903, and probably PS *Prince of Wales* which had been withdrawn from service in 1901.

Left: PS *Prince George* on Loch Lomond c.1905

Below: Disembarking at Ardlui Pier c.1908.

Bottom: a Caledonian Railway train from Glasgow on the platform at Balloch Pier as its passengers embark on the PS *Princess May* c.1906.

Top: PS *Wemyss Castle* taking on passengers at Leith's West Pier.

Middle: A busy steamer — probably the 384grt PS *Redgauntlet* built by Barclay, Curle & Co in 1895 — arriving at Aberdour's Stone Pier c.1910.

Bottom: Dominating the scene, MacBrayne's PS *Columba* disembarking passengers at Ardrishaig Pier, c.1900.

The 537grt PS *Waverley* — one of several vessels to carry that name — cruising in the Clyde estuary around 1905. This *Waverley* was built in 1899 by Inglis for the North British Railway Company, and in 1920 she was extensively remodelled, changing her profile considerably. She was lost at Dunkirk in May 1940.

The 1886-built PS *Madge Wildfire* actually carried two names associated with Scott in her 59-year life. As *Madge Wildfire* – a character from Scott's *Heart of Midlothian* – she sailed the Clyde lochs and, after being sold several times and sailing for many years on the South coast, she returned to Scotland in 1927 to sail on the Firth of Forth as the PS *Fair Maid*. Jeanie Deans, another character from *Heart of Midlothian*, gave her name to two much-loved steamers, and The Firth of Clyde Steam Packet Company operated the PS *Ivanhoe* for forty years from 1880 until 1920.

Long before the Second World War, the Clyde and West coast paddlers were being phased out, their roles taken over by more efficient turbine steamers. By the time services were resumed after the war, there were probably fewer than two

Below: Two unidentified small paddle tugs tied up at Methil in Fife c.1919. These small vessels usually worked as tugs, but occasionally also ran excursions in the summer. Larger vessels operated regular steamer services around the Fife coast and across the Firth of Forth to Leith, Granton and North Berwick. The two tugs seen here could be PS *The Earl*, built in South Shields in 1872, and 1905 Sunderland-built PS *Whitburn*, as both were stationed at Methil at the time.

Two views of PS *Queen of the South* (ex *Jeanie Deans*) at Southend Pier, and leaving Southend for Herne Bay in August 1966, during her brief life as an excursion steamer in the Thames estuary.

dozen still operational on the river. Less than two decades later, there were just a handful.

The 634grt PS *Jupiter*, built by Fairfield for the Caledonian Steam Packet Company in 1937 was withdrawn in 1961, and *Jeanie Deans* in 1964. The 544grt PS *Talisman* – the world's first diesel-electric powered excursion paddle steamer which had entered the water at Pointhouse in 1935 – survived until 17 November 1966, while PS *Caledonia*, built by Denny Brothers in 1934 followed her in 1969. That left *Waverley* as the only

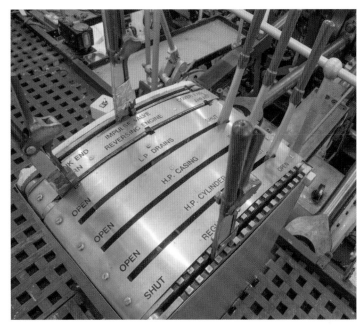

Left: The reconstructed control station in the engine room of PS *Maid of the Loch*.

Below left: As the era of the paddle steamer drew to a close, the Rankin & Blackmore engine fitted into PS *Maid of the Loch* in 1953 was of a design the company had been building for decades.

Below: The restored steam winch at Balloch slipway on Loch Lomond. The engine has been used to pull paddle steamers out of the water since 1902.

Right: The engine room telegraph, PS *Waverley*.

Below: The bridge telegraph, PS *Waverley*. The equipment was manufactured by Chadburns of Liverpool, a company whose name became so synonymous with ships' telegraphs that telegraphs were often referred to as 'chadburns', just as vacuum cleaners became known as 'hoovers'. The Chadburn Telegraph was first patented in 1870, and by 1898 the new company Chadburn's (Ship) Telegraph Ltd had been formed to manufacture the systems. The company's premises — and records — were destroyed by enemy bombing in May 1941, but the business was relocated to nearby Bootle, and by the time the telegraphs for PS *Waverley* were ordered, the makers were known as Chadburns (Liverpool) Ltd, and their beautifully designed dials, with their carefully tapered lettering, were considered a real sign of quality. There is still a great deal of interest in this equipment — so much so that there is a Chadburn Ships Telegraph Society, an aim of which is to fill in the gaps in the company's history.

Left: PS *Waverley* tied up at an unidentified quay in the 1980s.

Below left and below: The massive 1946-built double-ended Scotch boiler from PS *Waverley* is now exhibited outside the Scottish Maritime Museum's Linthouse Building at Irvine. The modifications made to it when the ship was converted from coal to oil are clearly evident. The ship was re-boilered in 1981, the original boiler being donated to the Royal Scottish Museum and displayed at Bo'ness before arriving at its present home.

paddle steamer on the river. Withdrawn in 1973, she is still sailing 40 years later.

PS *Jeanie Deans* had a brief stay of execution, being saved from the breakers' yard after her withdrawal from Clyde service, being bought by the London-based Coastal Steam Packet Company. Renamed PS *Queen of the South*, she was moved to the Thames for the 1966 and 1967 seasons. A great deal of work was undertaken to reverse the obvious signs of neglect she had experienced during her last months on the Clyde, but the move south was not a success and after two seasons she was moved to Antwerp in Belgium in December 1967 and broken up.

But while *Waverley* steamed on, in the case of *Caledonia*, any hopes that she too might be returned to steam under new colours were relatively short-lived. Initially sold for scrap, her new owners decided to try and keep her sailing. Renaming her *Old Caledonia*, the ship was put up for sale, but her new life turned out to be as a floating bar and restaurant rather than a working steamer. After a refit at Port Glasgow, she was moved to the Thames by her new owners, Bass Charrington, and moored on the Victoria Embankment near Waterloo Bridge.

After just eight years, the vessel was ravaged by fire on 27 April 1980 – a fire attended by two fire tender vessels and a number of fire engines – and was left beyond economic repair. She was towed to near Sittingbourne in Kent in the following month and broken up, finally leaving the valiant PS *Waverley* as the only Clyde excursion paddler still afloat.

All that survives of the PS *Caledonia* today are her engines, in storage and awaiting restoration, in a shed at Hollycombe Steam Collection in Liphook, Hampshire.

PS *Old Caledonia* in January 1977, five years after her move to the Victoria Embankment on the Thames following her refit at Lamont's shipyard in Port Glasgow. She had worked on the Clyde for five years before being requisitioned by the War Ministry in 1939, and serving as HMS *Goatfell* — including taking part in the Normandy landings — returning to Scotland in 1945 for a further 24 years.

Her final days — the vessel photographed from across the river on the morning of April 28 1980, smoke still billowing from her burned out superstructure, seven fire appliances still in attendance lined up along the Embankment, and a river fire tender tied up alongside.

Above: PS *Waverley* seen here sailing in the Solent in the 1980s. The restored and extensively rebuilt paddle steamer is a regular sight cruising around Britain's coast, visiting the Bristol Channel, the South coast, the coasts of Lancashire and North Wales, the North-east, and the West coast of her native Scotland – in fact most of the places where excursion steamers thrived in the heyday of the paddle steamer. As her paddles cannot be driven independently, she has a very large turning circle.

Left: In PS *Waverley's* surprisingly spacious engine room, Rankin & Blackmore's three-crank diagonal triple expansion engine, originally fed by coal-fired boilers, has been oil-fired since 1956.

137

STEAMERS TO SAIL ON, PLACES TO VISIT

PS *Kingswear Castle*
Dartmouth, Devon
www.dartmouthrailriver.co.uk
tel. 01803 555872
The 1924-built steamer offers river cruises, and scheduled sailings between Dartmouth and Totnes. The Dartmouth Steam Railway and Riverboat Company offers round trip tickets which include a journey from Kingswear to Paignton hauled by a vintage steam locomotive.

PS *Monarch*
Wareham Quay, Wareham, Dorset
tel. 07836 533022
The recently restored 1984-built 9grt steamer, with a passenger capacity of 12, is now based in Wareham, offering river cruises and charters.

PS *Waverley*
Lancefield Quay, Glasgow G3 8HA
www.waverleyexcursions.co.uk
tel. 0845 130 4647
The flagship of the Paddle Steamer Preservation Society, the restored 1947-built PS *Waverley* is a regular visitor to piers and harbours around Britain's coast. Full details of dates, times and locations of summer sailings, together with booking details, can be found on the Waverley Excursions website.

PS *Maid of the Loch*
The Pier, Balloch G83 8QX
www.maidoftheloch.com
tel. 01389 711865
Currently being restored on Loch Lomond, the 1953-built steamer is regularly open to visitors in the summer. Check website for details. The restored steam winch used to haul the steamer up the slipway for routine maintenance is in steam at selected times. The Loch Lomond Steamship Company plans eventually to return the *Maid* to steam.

PS *Charlotte Dundas*
MacKay Shipbuilders, Arbroath (no public access)

A three-quarter-size replica of the 1803 stern-wheeled PS *Charlotte Dundas*, was built in 1988 by the Cockenzie Boatyard & Slipway Co., and was briefly displayed at the Falkirk Wheel a few years ago. She now lies in an Arbroath shipyard, her future uncertain.

PS *Comet*
Greenock Rd, Town Centre, Port Glasgow PA14 5BP

The full size 1962 replica of Henry Bell's *Comet* stands near the waterfront adjacent to a supermarket car park. The replica is displayed in *Comet*'s original form – with two paddles in each paddle box. No longer operational, she is accessible at all times.

PS *Compton Castle*
Blackgang Chine Land of Imagination, IOW, PO38 2HN
www.blackgangchine.com
tel. 01983 730330

The much modified and almost unrecognisable steamer, minus her engine, is currently located in Truro, having been used as a floating restaurant, and later as a florist's shop. At the time of writing she is for sale. Her 1914 Cox & Co engine, however, is preserved and displayed at Blackgang Chine near Ventnor on the Isle of Wight.

PS *Empress*
In the former Southampton Maritime Museum's collection was the engine from the 1879-built Cosens steamer PS *Empress*. When the steamer was decommissioned in 1955 after 76 years of service, this was the last oscillating steam engine still operational in Britain. The Maritime Museum is now closed, and the engine, having been deemed too heavy to be moved to the new Sea City Museum, is currently inaccessible and looking for a home.

PS *John H Amos*
Medway Maritime Trust, Chatham
www.medwaymaritimetrust.org.uk
tel. 07710 900004

The 1931 Paisley-built paddle tug is currently being restored on the pontoon *Portal Narvik* in Chatham Historic Dockyard.

PS *Medway Queen*
Gillingham, Kent ME7 1RX
www.medwayqueen.co.uk
tel. 01634 575717
Currently being refitted on the Medway, there are plans eventually to return the 1924 steamer and Dunkirk veteran, built by Ailsa Shipbuilding of Troon, to service. This is really a rebuild rather than a restoration, as a completely new hull has been manufactured in Bristol, and the original engine and fitments retro-fitted.

PS *Princess Elizabeth*
Rue De La Collinière, Dunkerque, France
Limited public access, but viewable from quayside
Another Dunkirk veteran paddle steamer, built in Southampton by Day, Summers & Co., PS *Princess Elizabeth* is now used as a conference centre, moored adjacent to the Pole Marine shopping centre in the port area of Dunkerque. To meet the demands of her current role, her elegant profile – as seen here in 1960 – has been somewhat compromised. Her engine was removed long ago.

PS *Tattershall Castle*
Victoria Embankment, London SW1A 2HR
www.thetattershallcastle.co.uk
tel. 07584 680 1867
Now a floating bar and restaurant, the 1934-built former Humber ferry, although much modified over the years, still has her original engine. It is just visible through glass panels into her unlit engine room. Her paddles were removed after a major refurbishment in 2004, and sadly not even the painted decoration of the paddle boxes remains

PS *Wingfield Castle*
Jackson Dock, Maritime Avenue, Hartlepool TS24 0XZ
www.hartlepoolsmaritimeexperience.com
tel. 01429 860077
After a time on the Thames, the former Humber ferry, built by William Gray of Hartlepool in 1934, is one of the centrepieces, along with HMS *Trincomalee*, of the Hartlepool Maritime Experience. Her engine, built by Gray's Central Marine Engine Works, is in situ and there is free public access to most parts of the vessel.

Brunel's SS *Great Britain*
Great Western Dockyard, Bristol BS1 6TY
www.ssgreatbritain.org
tel. 0117 926 0680

Although Brunel's great 1843 transatlantic liner was launched as a screw-propelled steamer, she was originally conceived and designed as a paddler. Thomas Guppy's huge engine was simply turned through 90° and connected to the propellor shaft by a chain drive. The replica of Guppy's low pressure engine installed in the beautifully restored ship is typical of a design installed in a number of early paddle steamers.

Glasgow Riverside Museum
100 Pointhouse Place, Glasgow G3 8RS
www.glasgowlife.org.uk/museums/pages/home.aspx
tel. 0141 287 2720

The museum stands on the site of A. & J. Inglis's Pointhouse Yard where many of the great Clyde paddlers were built – including surviving steamers PS *Waverley* and PS *Maid of the Loch*. There are some fine ship models, and other material relating to Glasgow's shipbuilding heritage.

Felixstowe Museum
Viewpoint Road, Felixstowe, Suffolk IP11 3TW
www.felixstowemuseum.org
tel. 01394 674355

The museum has a dedicated 'Paddle Steamer Room' containing artefacts from Belle Steamers and other East coast paddle steamer operators. Many of the items on display are on loan from the Paddle Steamer Preservation Society's extensive collection.

Hollycombe Steam Collection
Iron Hill, Liphook, Hampshire GU30 7LP
www.hollycombe.co.uk
tel. 01428 724900

The triple expansion engine from the PS *Caledonia*, built in 1934 by Denny Brothers for the Caledonian Steam Packet Company, was rescued after the 1980 fire on the former Clyde steamer and is now awaiting preservation at Hollycombe. Viewable on request.

Markham Grange Steam Museum

Long Lands Lane, Brodsworth, South Yorkshire DN5 7XD
www.markhamgrangesteammuseum.co.uk
tel. 01302 330430

The museum's 1907 'grasshopper' side lever engine by Hepple & Sons of South Shields was the port engine of the steam tug *Old Trafford* and is preserved here together with its paddle. This was a 19th century design with more in common with a beam engine than a contemporary steamship engine.

National Maritime Museum

Romney Road, Greenwich, London SE10 9NF
www.rmg.co.uk
tel. 020 8858 4422

The National Maritime Museum is *the* museum for anything to do with shipping and maritime history. On display and worked now by electricity, is the starboard engine from the steam tug *Old Trafford/Reliant*. The tug was dismantled by the museum in 1999.

Scottish Maritime Museum, Dumbarton

Castle Street, Dumbarton, Dunbartonshire G82 1QS
www.scottishmaritimemuseum.org
tel. 01294 278283

The 1823 side-lever engine designed by Robert Napier for the PS *Leven* is on display outdoors at the Scottish Maritime Museum's Dumbarton site. It is now displayed outside the Denny Ship Model Experiment Tank.

Scottish Maritime Museum, Irvine

Harbour Road, Irvine, Ayrshire KA12 8QE
www.scottishmaritimemuseum.org
tel. 01294 278283

The Irvine site includes many detailed paddle steamer models, marine steam engines, and other artefacts, displayed in the rebuilt Linthouse Engine Shop dating from 1872, where the steam engines for many fine vessels were constructed. The building, from the Linthouse yard of Alexander Stephen & Sons in Govan, was re-erected on the Irvine site in the 1980s. PS *Waverley*'s original 1946 boiler stands outside.

INDEX
Page numbers in italics denote illustrations